Out of the Darkness: A Survivor's Story

Alice Jay

Out of the Darkness: A Survivor's Story

Cover design: Creativelogoart

ISBN: 978-1-937400-48-4
ISBN: 978-1-937400-49-1 ebook

Printed in the United States of America

Published by Manifold Grace Publishing House, LLC
Southfield, Michigan 48033
www.manifoldgracepublishinghouse.com

Dedications

This book is dedicated to people who can help those who were trafficked recover, to educate and enlighten those sheltered from the realities of the life.

To those who are safe and sound in the comfort of their homes, grateful for NOT having this experience.

To survivors so they will not lose the will to live. We strengthen survivors by providing tools.

To professionals/sheltered/survivors/agnostics; those too educated to believe. To survivors who often don't know any other way of life. Finally, to those who refuse to believe in God, I would have had no way out – but God.

Acknowledgments

Thank you! To everyone I have ever known simply because knowing you - made me. The woman I am today is full of strength and courage hoping for a better future.

Thanks to God for sustaining me with His grace and mercy.

Thanks to all my family and friends.

Special thanks to: Edward Johnson (my brother) and Darlynn Johnson (not related) for your contributions. You made the editing and publishing possible.

Thank you Alison Bedker, Darlene Dickson. If it had not been for your belief in me, this book would still be sitting on the shelf.

Thanks to Saurice Grady. Raynad Smith, Jessica Mays, April Wright, Rhonda Dhummas, and Irene Garza for all your love and support. I could not have made a comeback without you!

Last, but not least, thanks to the House of Metamorphosis, the San Diego Rescue Mission and Detroit World Outreach.

Table of Contents

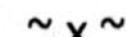

Foreword

I have been blessed to know Alice Johnson for the past 11 years. We are family by marriage, but I had only heard stories of her for years before we met. The stories were not pretty, they had no happy endings. Our family has always been acutely aware of the struggles and trauma that she suffered. I recall one story that had me feeling particularly intimidated, but despite the family dysfunction she remains fiercely protective of her family. So when a girl showed up one day where Alice was hanging out with a few of her brothers and began playing one against the other, causing a fight, Alice chased her off down the street... literally... with a barbell. Like I said, intimidating.

I would hear stories laced with sadness of when Alice tried to come back home and her sister opened her home to her. Alice could not handle the four walls, rules, schools. She had been alone for so long, finally seeking solace in an environment she thought would be stable. Suffice it to say, Alice did not find peace or solace. The love was there, but sometimes that is not enough. Especially when one is trying to heal from such trauma.

When we finally met I was surprised at how easily she laughed and how deeply she loved. After hearing pieces of her story throughout the years, I imagined a hard and scarred individual; that was not Alice. Through it all, Alice has been honest and open about her story. She was the first person I ever heard use the term Human Trafficking. Imagine the shock of hearing of such a horrible thing from one of your own family, knowing they experienced it. That was my experience with Alice. She sat in her sister's living room talking to me, her "new niece," telling me of being held at gun point and raped. She spoke in Japanese and told us of being trafficked to Hawaii.

It is hard to visualize Alice so broken and weak, but she will paint the picture for you. I remember the night she left us. We were crying. She was screaming that she needed us to help her. We were as powerless as she was. It is painful to tell someone you care about, that you cannot help them anymore until they help themselves. Alice continued on her journey. We waited. Words can only begin to express the pride I feel to see her shine today. She has opened her heart up to the world, leaving her darkest secrets out for scrutiny.

Since the first time I met her, she made it clear, her goal was to allow herself to heal enough to help others who have been victims of Human Trafficking. Now, not only is she helping others, she is working to prevent more people from experiencing the same trauma. She has spoken in front of State Representatives of Michigan to push for changes in the law that will not allow perpetrators to get off the hook. She has spoken in front of several groups of women, men and young people to educate them regarding the issue of Human Trafficking. Now she is going further to organize fundraisers for people in need. She began this endeavor with many obstacles from the start.

As a victim of Human Trafficking she was robbed of an education most Americans take for granted. She started her mission as a single mother which is a challenge in and of itself. Nothing, not trauma, lack of education, poverty or raising a family, has held Alice back. What a glorious thing it is to see this change come to fruition in our generation. Human Trafficking has been a horrendous blight on our world for far too long! Join me in lifting up this voice that will help the movement end this tragedy!

In her story, Alice speaks for millions of women and children throughout the course of our history who have been robbed of a voice to speak; wrecked and left for dead. This book will educate our world so we can move forward in this fight to end Human Trafficking. The first step is acknowledging the problem, then learning about it and finally, taking a stand to end it.

Jessica Mays
December 14, 2014

Introduction

This is a true story based on my life experience. It is not just another survivor's story; it is the story of a journey to spiritual growth. After being abducted as a child and exploited through the underground world of human trafficking, I wanted to know why God loved all the children in the world but me. This is a testimony about a girl with hopes and dreams; who loved the Lord and loved life. Then one day her hopes and dreams were gone. She was lost and turned out. Dead to the world - will she ever recover? Is there a way out?

This is the cold hard reality of human trafficking. It is not a book about statistical theory; it is the raw uncut survival story of a child of the night. It is the raw reality of my experiences overcoming the world of human trafficking. Some of the language is raw too. I changed most of it because I no longer speak that way; it was, however, the language of my world.

Anyone who reads this book will benefit and be changed forever. There are 20 years of personal research in this book. What you know about this way of life is simply a myth. Layers and layers of a life style that has been misinterpreted for centuries will be unveiled. We will lay the myths to rest for this book is based on my life experience.

This is my gift to the world and I hope you will be pleased. The names and dates have been changed to protect the innocent and the not so innocent. This is my truth; my light. I invite the professionals, parents, young adults, atheists and agnostics to come walk and talk awhile with me as I reveal the darkest moments of my life.

May your eyes be opened that you receive comfort in trouble and peace through your storms!

~ One ~

Where I Come From

I am the youngest girl of 12 children and I grew up in a very poor home; every man for himself. There was always a lot of chaos, fighting and arguing. Neglect, incest and abuse was the norm in that household. I adjusted to my surroundings as all my sisters and brothers did. Being an introvert who learned how to hide very well and how to fight by the age of five, never stopped me from dreaming or playing and having fun with my brothers. I loved dancing and writing songs. I liked climbing trees and going to church. I was a good student who loved school and loved to learn. Always ahead of my class, I was better at everything than anyone I knew.

School and church were kind of an escape from the chaos in my house. I really liked the snacks and lunches best of all. I remember always trying to make the best of my surroundings, and trying to stay low on the radar not to cause my mother any trouble.

The first time I remember being abused was when my father threw me from the attic window and the next door neighbor lady caught me. My mother said it was because I was hiding in the attic crying. She said when she found me and asked me why, I said to her that I was talking to my grandfather and he said something bad was going to happen to me. When she told my father, he called me a witch and threw me out of the window. As I look back now I realize that I was blessed and highly favored. I, like my grandfather - a

Blackfoot Indian spiritual leader, was a very spiritual person.

Once my mother and father got divorced, things got worse. It was normal for me to go without things like hot water or food. I rarely got new clothes and if I did, they were hand-me-downs. Kids were cruel and called me names. At first I tried to pay them no mind and just be the best I could be. Once the divorce was final, my mom got a new boyfriend.

I always felt sorry for the abuse my mother and brothers received from him. I also envied my brothers; they were her favorites. It was very obvious that my mom and her boyfriend liked them better than me, just because they were boys. He worked them like mules. He had them chop down a one hundred year old oak tree. My fourteen-year-old brother got the worst of it! He was white with blonde hair and blue eyes. The other boys were seven, five and four years old. He worked them day in and day out, chopping down trees and, stuff like that. My mother paid no attention when he would strip us naked and beat us with his belt buckle. If one got it, we all got it. He didn't beat me as bad as the boys – my dad would have killed him. After his business started rolling, he was gone.

Around this time I became anorexic. My mother acted like it was a personal attack against her. She became violent, especially towards me. She would often scream at me saying, "You look just like your father!" Other times she would line us up on the couch, screaming about how much she hated us. She usually stared directly at me. I would have preferred her to do the usual banging my head into the wall, than to hear her screaming those words while jumping up and down like a crazy maniac.

When my mother got a new boyfriend, you could tell because she was happy. She would get all dressed up to go out for an evening. I always thought my mother was so beautiful. I wished that I looked like her instead of my father. No one dared question my mother. She was rarely happy as it was, so no one dared say anything to break her spirit.

When I was about eight I remember my mother seemed a little uneasy and desperate. She told me her friend was coming to take me shopping for some new shoes. I didn't understand why she picked me over my brothers. She dressed me up in my Sunday best, then sent me off with some stranger she'd met at the local pool hall. He did take me shopping at Kmart and he bought me some Hush Puppy shoes. We went back to his apartment. This was a rundown building where hookers and junkies hung out. The building stood across the street from the projects. It was the kind of building that you have to share the bathroom with everyone in the building.

He sat me on his lap and put my new shoes on my feet. Then he started rubbing my upper thigh. He went inside my panties molesting me. I started crying. He kept saying my name. He told me I was going to be his little whore.

He had been drinking beer the whole time. When he got up to use the bathroom in the sink, I shot out the door as fast as I could. I could hear him calling me. When I looked back, there was a man who had to be in his forties, holding himself, laughing loudly. I ran home about ten blocks. By the time I made it home, I was faint and frantic. I told my mother what happened and she became enraged.

She started crying and screaming, "You liar, you lying little whore! He loves me, not you!" She began banging my head into the wall, screaming how she hated me. Then she threw me in the closet and left me there for hours in the dark. I could not and would not speak of it to anyone because I didn't want to offend my mother, even though I didn't know what whore meant. I just felt she hated me, so I began to hate her. She would never regain my trust or respect. I began to hate and resent her for being my mother. I told her I wish I had a black mother, she laughed.

We moved out of the old neighborhood into a predominantly white neighborhood on the northeast side of town. There was a mixed couple next door that my mother knew from my father. He would be the next man to molest me. I remember my mother leaving me with him. He told me to sit on the floor then sat across from me. He started telling me he had a daughter named Alice, too. He kept asking me if I understood. I began to cry. He told me not to cry, saying he wouldn't hurt me, and to think about ice cream. That is all I can remember. I was still eight years old. Even at that young age I knew I was being disrespected. When he started touching me, I mentally and emotionally went somewhere else, to escape any physical pain that I might have to feel. They call it disassociation, something I mastered at a very young age. It was a gift to me. I knew I couldn't tell my mother. I didn't want another episode like the last one.

I went to school in the neighborhood that fall. I always thought that I was an average kid, but at this school no one would play with me. Even the Mexican boy turned to me and said, "I don't want to play with you, nigger." That was the first time I experienced prejudice and discrimination. Later on that day, the woman next door broke the news that they were moving. The KKK came to our house saying. "Nigger lovers must go!" My mother badmouthed them saying: "My son is a black panther and I'll have your white asses fucked up." The next morning there was a small cross burning on our front lawn. My mother decided it was best that we move back to the southwest side of town, since there was no man around.

We didn't stay there long before we moved again to a hotel where my mother's ex-boyfriend lived, the one who urinated in the sink and molested me. The place was run down and raggedy. There were drunks and hookers in and out all day long. They all thought my brothers and me were so cute. The hobos would give us change; the hookers gave us dollars and let my brothers feel on their breasts. The pimps gave us weed and toys or candy. We learned a lot about hustling from them. Sometimes they would stop us and give us lectures on surviving in the world. Other times we would just listen to the pimps while they got their shoes shined at the local barbershop. Soon we moved again, deep on the west side. This is where I would go to the fourth and fifth grade.

That spring I went to Memphis with my father's sister, Aunt Stella. She was so strong and beautiful, all three hundred pounds of her. She cooked me cobbler and greens.

Aunt Stella just loved me to death. I wished I never had to leave.

By now I was in the rebellious stage. I got caught smoking cigarettes and was disciplined. So I ran away to my cousin's house where he molested me. I told my Aunt and she took me back home to Michigan. I arrived back home that summer. My mother introduced her new boyfriend to me as her husband. They got married about a week after I got back. She wanted me to call him daddy. I hated her for that. She had just met him three months earlier.

I hated her most for giving him our food stamp money for alcohol. I hated not having clean clothes or hot water, roaches everywhere, and mice jumping out of my cereal box. I hated him for beating my mother, my brothers, and me like we stole something when we had done absolutely nothing wrong. I hated going to church on Sunday morning just to be beaten on Sunday evening. He tried to molest my best friend one day, when she came to my house to visit me. I couldn't play with her anymore. I hated being in the house because of all the violence.

Most of my days were spent disassociated in a dreamland trying to escape my reality. I would hide away in my room and rock on my bed for hours at a time, dreaming. Dreaming I was somewhere else and someone else. I hated my life. I would be so afraid at night. I couldn't get out of the bed to use the bathroom and I didn't feel safe in my house. I used to like being outside in the fields. Once, I found a field with trees shading an open space. So I made it mine. I put up chairs, rugs, and drapes that I had found. I built a clubhouse where I would go and write music and sing.

One day, I ran home from school to find police surrounding my block. Someone was dead. There was a young black man in my neighborhood who had been teaching me karate, his prostitute had stabbed him. People were screaming, "She killed my brother!" Policemen were trying to detain them. I ran to my secret spot of serenity. Lo and behold, there was my baby brother running behind me. I tried to lose him because I didn't want him to find my hideout. He cried and promised not to tell, so I let him come with me.

We heard crying as we approached my hideout. Our eyes widened as we saw a naked woman. She had long brown hair, and was curled up in a ball on my rug. She told us to go get the police. My brother ran to get them. I stayed with her. Blood was dripping down her face. It was everywhere. I was confused and wanted to help, but I didn't know how. I remembered she was a local streetwalker, and a friend of my sister. My brother came back with the police and the officer told us we had to leave because this was no place for children.

I am not sure if she lived or died. I just see her sitting there crying and bleeding. My family and I moved again shortly after that. I was nine years old at the time.

One evening, my friend from school invited me to her house. We were playing dolls in her room and got thirsty, so she went to get us some Kool-Aid. Suddenly her two uncles walked into the room and turned out the lights. I was very scared and started screaming. The girl I was visiting with was on the other side of the door crying and screaming, "Stop! Leave my friend alone!" She tried to open the door but they pushed her down and told her to go downstairs. They took off the doorknob and then they raped me.

I was crying. I tried to fight! They were just too big. I shut down, not even remembering the violent act. I was back in the room and they just ran away laughing! I ran out of there as fast as I could. My mother saw the blood dripping down my legs. She started screaming, "Rape! They raped my baby!" It seemed as though every kid in the neighborhood was outside playing.

Charges were dropped because my brother shot and killed their dog. It was on the news and everyone knew that I had been raped. Even though we moved back to my old neighborhood and I switched schools, people still knew and kids were still mean; as kids can be. I felt as if I did something wrong. By this time, I not only hated my life, I hated everyone else too. I became very angry and would fight a lot. Every time I got a chance I would hurt someone. By this time in my life I felt that I was born bad, which got me kicked out of all the public schools in the city. I started going to an alternative school where I smoked weed and drank every chance I got.

Right around this time my mother caught me drunk and high off weed. She attempted to assault me while I was high. As usual she grabbed me by my hair and attempted to bang my head into the wall. After a couple times of that, I reached out and snatched her up by the neck, slamming her against the wall. I told her if she ever touched me again I would kill her. She insisted I leave her house immediately. So I did. I stayed with friends. I stayed with my oldest sister a lot. She was married with a new baby so I tried not to be a thorn in her side. I would go there at night if I couldn't find anywhere else to stay. I was still trying to go to school.

My brother and I were very close; we loved to hustle the pimps, bums and hoes. We would snatch racks of meat off the meat trucks delivering to the local stores. We would snatch bags of groceries and run. Then we started breaking into cars going for joy rides, taking the radios and selling them. We would hang out until the early morning hours trying to figure out the safest place for me to lay my head.

We came up with another get rich quick scheme, we pretended to hitchhike and hustle the drivers to give us a ride or money. Once there was a young man with blonde hair and blue eyes. I can't forget him because he was the first person to pull a gun on me. We ran as fast and hard as we could, hiding behind the liquor store. Scared we waited until we found someone to buy for us. We downed a fifth of Wild Irish Rose, then continued walking across town, stumbling and staggering the whole way.

The police came and took him to Boy's Training School. When my mother found out what happened she blamed me. I went home to see my mother and use the phone. She started yelling at me. "You're not my daughter. You're a disgrace to this family. Don't dare show your face around here! I never want to see you again. Don't dare show your face around here, not even at my funeral!"

~ Two ~

The Streets

When my oldest sister heard what happened she came over, snatched the phone from me and started hitting me with it. I had a forty-ounce glass bottle of malt liquor that I smacked her across the face with. She blocked it with her arm. The shattered glass cut her face and fractured her arm. I was sorry I hurt her. It was too late.

The police came and took me to juvenile detention where I was charged with assault. They released me to my mother with probation. As soon as I got home my mother insisted that I get out. I was not allowed back in my mother's house at all after this. I was really on my own now and had no other choice but to take my place as a gangster.

The Black Gangster Disciples were a local gang in my neighborhood. I heard they were recruiting and I needed somewhere to live, some type of family. There were three of us who tried out. I was known for my skills and my badass behavior. It was two dark skinned girls and me who showed up that day for tryouts. They were a year or two older than me so I thought I didn't have a chance with my high yellow behind. My skin was so white, most of the time I had to fight just to prove I was black. We were kind of friends from elementary school. They asked us who the Kings were, I knew them. They asked us who could make a six point, which was their gang sign. I did. They had us fight each other. At the end of the initiation I was the only one standing. I didn't miss a beat. I was the strongest, hardest and most desperate kid there. I wasn't leaving, because I had nowhere to go. We lived in a big house, somebody's Granddad's or something. They gave me an angel to watch over me. His name was Break. He was meaner than me. If I went somewhere he went with me. I got tired of him following me around every day! One day I lost him. I went out to try and hustle some food to bring back. I just wanted the chance to prove myself. Everybody had a job to do but me! I was the youngest queen.

They called gangster girls, Queens. I had been spotted hanging out by the gay bar. I was ordered not to leave the house for my own safety without a disciple with me. I couldn't do anything and I wasn't expected to either. I mostly just watched the house. I learned how to shoot a pistol and a sawed off shotgun. I cleaned the house and ordered food, got rid of weapons and counted money. As soon as I got comfortable there; the house got raided and everything fell apart overnight. Away from my family, the Disciples gone; I was alone and hungry.

I started hanging out at the place called "The Island" where junkies and hookers dwelled. I was reintroduced to the game at "The Island." Deep up in the sewer I met a heroin addict named Scarface Will. He had just got out of the penitentiary after doing fifteen years for murder. They called him Scarface because he had burns over his face and body from paint thinner. I never asked him about it. He had his own place there and let me stay with him. He never disrespected me and tried to take care of me. People would be coming in and out, shooting dope all day long. They call these places "shooting galleries." Most of the people were nice to me. Others wouldn't even acknowledge my presence. I'd do the usual breaking in cars and robbing people for food and money.

One day my friend Will left to get some dope for some people waiting. I was sitting there watching this junkie trying to hit himself. He had lumps all up and down his body. He injected the dope into his body, and started to moan. I felt I wanted that, so I asked him to give me some. He did not hesitate to tie the rubber on my arm. A couple more people were hanging around. There was a local hooker in her forties with no teeth. She said, "Don't do that! This is Will's niece." He said that he would only give me a little bit. As he pulled the syringe up and brought it towards my arm, Will walked through the door. He right away dropped the bag he was carrying and screamed, "No! What the fuck are you doing?" He gave everyone their things screaming, "Get your shit and get out! I want everybody out!" As I reached for my things, he grabbed my hand and said "Not you Alice."

When everyone was gone he explained to me about the casualties of using the syringe. He talked about Hepatitis A, B and C. Then he asked me if I was ready to die and talked to me about HIV and AIDS. He told me "If someone sticks a needle in your arm, they're trying to kill you! He used this metaphor: Say someone is drunk. They start hitting you and beating you up. Do you know what you got to do? You have to kill them before they kill you. He said when people are drunk and high they will hurt you. They don't care about you! This dope will take you there, to the point of no return. They won't even remember they did it the next day. It's poison girl! You're going to have to learn to protect yourself out here on these streets. I'm not always going be around to save you," while he injected dope into his arm.

I didn't want to hear that. I just wanted to try it once. There was a knock on the door. It was a mutual friend. A white boy named Jamie who was seventeen. He also tried explaining to me that this was no place for a child. Jamie said if I started getting high at eleven years old. I would never live to see seventeen. He came in with his syringe and his dope. I asked, "Why are you letting him get high here?" Will sent him into the bathroom. Then turned to me, whispering in my ear, "He is already dead." When Jamie came out the bathroom I was still trying to convince Will I could handle it. After he finished his hit he was more than willing to hit me. He told Will, "You can't stop her. It is better you let her get high here with us rather than out there on the streets." Will asked, "Do you have a clean syringe? I'm not giving her one of mine."

Jamie said, "Oh, you can't use mine either." There was another knock at the door. A man walked in with a bag of clean syringes. There was no stopping me now! Will went in the room and closed the door. Jamie wrapped the rubber around my arm and injected dope in my arm with the syringe. From this point on I continued to shoot dope every chance I got, for the next year. I had become desperate and strung out. I went to my mother for help. Coming down was the hardest thing. I would have rather slit someone's throat than endure that type of torture. My mother said that she knew what I was doing because people told her about me. She said I was not her daughter anymore. She said she couldn't raise her family with me around so the least I could do was leave the state. She didn't have to see me or hear about me. I grabbed a rug cutter and threatened to take her life. My baby brother tried to stop me. After I dropped kicked him in the back, he ran and called the police. The police called an ambulance.

It took several of them to restrain me. I was sent to a mental hospital and released two weeks later. I was home just long enough to grab my things and leave. Will got busted and was back in jail! Jamie just disappeared! I never shot dope without them before. I wasn't going to start either.

I slept in public bathrooms and in abandoned buildings for a while. When I found myself starving for food and in need of clothing, I continued my hustle to survive. Once I saw a pretty young lady, she wasn't from around here and looked out of place.

She was by herself leaning against the car door of a bad ass two tone brown Continental. I approached her and put on my mean face. I said, "You got some money for me! What are you doing in my neighborhood?"

She said, "You don't want to mess with me little girl. See this car? It belongs to my pimp."

I said, "I don't care about your pimp! I'm going to take his car, too."

She began to laugh saying "He will kill you little girl."

~ Three ~

Abduction and Exploitation

I saw a handsome Mexican crossing the street. She told me to get away from the car. I knew this would be out of my league, so I stepped back. She got in his car. They talked briefly. She got out of the car, handed me twenty dollars and took my picture. A couple of weeks later I was walking down to the public pool with my friends. We saw that Continental again. We went to take a closer look to see if we could take it. Not knowing that we were about to meet Satan himself. There came this Mexican running towards us with a loaded pistol. He saw me and started to laugh. He yelled up to the window of the two story yellow house saying, "Baby it's your little friend. Come see!" They called him Ricco! He was scary yet beautiful in an exciting way. Ricco had long black wavy hair with a strong built body. My friend and I looked at each other and ran off as fast as we could to the local swimming pool and went swimming.

We decided to take a different route home and leave them Mexicans alone. I ended up going to juvenile for being out past curfew. My friend's mother wouldn't let me stay at her house. She said I was probably a runaway. It was ironic to me how you could be a runaway if your mom kicked you out. I never understood how they didn't care that I had nowhere to live, just that I was a runaway. My second oldest sister finally came and got me. I was supposed to stay with her in the suburbs. Around this time, I was angry at the world. I recall hating everything and everybody: strangers, my life, etc. I became rebellious, and had no rules. I could not stay with my sister. I couldn't bear to see the abuse that she endured from her husband. So I ran away, back to the streets. I started going to the high schools and breaking in to have somewhere to sleep. Once again I slept anywhere, bus stations, abandoned buildings, etc. I bought clothes or stole them. I drank alcohol every chance I got; but no drugs.

One day I was attempting to get inside because it was getting late. I knew I would go back to juvenile if the police spotted me so I was walking really fast. I noticed a car swerve up next to me with two men in it. They started yelling, "Come here, come here!" I ran as fast as I could. Two more cars hit the corner as soon as I turned it. I tried to dash behind the building and hit the fence. As soon as I touched the fence I heard, "We will shoot you! Stop, come here, come here!" As I turned around I saw six men. Three cars and several guns were pointed at me, pistols and AK 14's. They blocked me in behind an abandoned building and forced me to choose to go with one of them. I had never seen them before. I was scared for my life. Then I saw Ricco. He called out to me.

He was leaning against the two-tone Lincoln with his arms crossed, just observing. He was the Mexican guy with the long beautiful wavy hair. I went to him because he wasn't pointing a pistol in my face. I thought I was being saved. He bought me beautiful clothes. He told me I was beautiful, and he said he loved me. I don't think I ever felt so safe and loved. Little did I know that he arranged the whole thing! It was two weeks before my 12th birthday that I would be initiated into a life of prostitution. First, I was stripped naked in the middle of a graveyard in the dead of winter where I was raped at gunpoint. He locked me in the basement with his pit bull for a couple of days then commanded me to start hoeing on the street corner. I was scared and crying, "No, no, let me go, I hate you! I hate you!"

There were several methods used to reform me. If I spoke about my family, he would slap me over and over saying my family member's names - one by one. He continued until my tears turned to blood and my ears were ringing, until I would cry out "Please, okay!"

If I refused to perform, he would put lit cigarettes out on me or throw lit matches at my face and dare me to cry. He would rape me at night and wake me up with a board in the morning. If I talked about God, he would kick me in my stomach until I couldn't breathe and ask me, "Where is your God now?" When he would take my breath away, he would proclaim that he was God. I was not allowed to breathe unless he allowed me too. After about five months or so of this, I was willing to submit. I felt I had no choice. I felt I owed him for taking care of me. He said I would die on the streets if I left him. He said he saved me and I started convincing myself that he did.

I was a slave at twelve years old! I had heard about slavery. I knew if I didn't obey him I would die. I didn't understand why these men would line up, ten to fifteen cars in a row! Waiting to have their way with me! I would cry silently as they lay over me sweating and breathing. I felt like a human toilet. I hated my life. There were a couple of police officers who knew what was going on. They came to the house.

The police turned their heads as if I wasn't even there because he was paying them off. I hated being on the streets. People were so cruel and mean. They drove by and cursed at me. Some of them threw eggs and pennies at me; some would get out of their cars and assault me. They didn't care if I was a child. They just hated me and wanted to hurt me. One day I came home there was a young boy there about ten named Tony. Ricco had recruited him as a young dope dealer and gunman. He said he wanted to stay. I begged Ricco to let him go. He would laugh and say go where.

Ricco decided I was two young for the streets. I overheard one of the officers tell him "She can't be out here like this; you're going to have to send her away!" He would have the other girls go out and bring the johns to the house. The other girls got mad because it messed with their quarters and complained because I didn't have to work. One day he brought home another girl. She was two years older than me. She was a beautiful black girl with caramel skin and light eyes. She had full lips and an hourglass body. We called her Suzie. We had so much fun together or so we thought. Then there came Sasha. She was the same age as me. She was mixed like me, light skinned with long hair. We would do each other's make up, covering the bruises on each other's faces. We comforted each other and looked out for each other.

It was just us four now. I didn't know where the other girls went. I didn't dare ask either, none of us did. Every day was very busy and exciting. I was now 14 years old. Sasha was twelve almost 13. Suzie was 15. Young Tony was 12 years old. We were always on the block hustling twenty hours a day. How was it that we were not recognized by the police or anyone in civil society? We all looked as young as we were, or younger. We were selling dope and everything else. I tried to run away every chance I got but there just weren't a lot of places to hide in our small town. Ricco had a lot of connections and would always find me. I never dared to go to the police for fear of my life. I had seen Ricco hurt people, he had hurt me. The street code was very clear "snitches get stitches". I didn't want anyone I loved to be hurt. He decided that each of us girls would go to a brothel. Together we were too strong for him. He sent Suzie to New York. Sasha was sent to Chicago, and I was sent to New Orleans.

This house I distinctly remember. The madam was an old white lady who practiced witchcraft. She tried to convince me to have sex with her clients without condoms. Yet my knowledge of the game was embedded deep. I was much too smart for that. We would come back with thousands of dollars. We went all over the country. Once we were checked in we weren't allowed to come back out until our time was up. He would make the arrangements so we hardly knew where we were going. We would be escorted to the bus station or airport, given a ticket with a destination and once we got there someone would be waiting for us. They would ask us to lie down so we never knew where we were going.

Whoever represented you dictated how long you would

be there. We were not allowed to leave or go outside. We were not allowed to use the phones or watch television. We were not allowed to talk to each other really. These places were always dark and had no windows. One way in and no way out. There would be a bar for you to go sit in and drink until a customer came. Then we would line up and he would choose one. We had no clothes except for the ones we came in with. We were only allowed to wear lingerie. I heard other girls crying or being hit. We were only allowed to come out when the men came to choose one of us.

I paid an older woman to give me some other numbers. Men would line up and take numbers to have their way with us. I would lay there disconnected from any type of feelings or emotions. Dreaming of a different life! The men who came in these places were educated businessmen, the typical middle-aged white male. The others were Italians and other foreigners from Korea, Japan, the Middle East, Australia, and Mexico! There were some black men, not very many though.

I cannot remember addresses or streets. I was usually told to lie down. These were places of business. They took ATM cards. They had cash registers. They were disguised as hotels, massage parlors, bathhouses and strip joints. Some were just local residences. Some were located in small country towns. Others were in major cities. I remember being in North and South Carolina, Tampa, New York, Alaska, Bahamas, Hawaii, Denver, Detroit and Portland, Oregon.

One time I came back. Suzie had returned earlier than I did. Ricco sent her out there by herself on the streets. She was stabbed fourteen times by a school teacher. I wanted to leave, but I had no place to go. When I came back home, there was no Sasha either. I overheard Ricco saying that Sasha was shot in the head at the house in Chicago. I never saw her again. What I did see was young Tony strung out on crack. He was infatuated with the game and the hustle. I was climbing out of the window trying to escape. Young son, little Tony strung out on crack had an AK-14 at my head. He told me to get back inside, or he was going to kill me. I sat in my room reading a bible I had picked up at one of the brothels where I had been that was disguised as a hotel. Ricco came in the room. I slid my bible up under the bed.

He sat next to me and leaned in to kiss me. I must have shown some sign of disgust because he was upset. He said "You ugly half-breed! I give you everything! I buy you beautiful clothes. I buy you jewelry that you never wear. If you want to eat lamb, I would go kill one for you! I saved your life. You were dying on those streets. Where was your God when you were dying? You whore, where was your God when you were putting that needle in your arm? It was me that saved you! Me!" He got up and called for the other women. New women I had never seen before who worked for him came in my room.

He would find these girls out on the streets. They would stay with him for a while. He never kept the older ones very long. I couldn't figure out how they could just leave. He never let them talk to me very much. He would always get mad. This time he let them beat me up. All six of them started punching and kicking me. This time I fought back as hard as I could. I heard him screaming "get her." Then I heard the girls saying "Grab her arms." I felt someone grabbing my arms and another one jumping on my back. I hit the ground as they stomped me and kicked me. I finally began to cry.

Ricco said, "Enough, let's go!" as they walked out the door. I was staring at the Bible Ricco dropped in front of me, hearing him ask me, "Why didn't your God save you!"

I overheard someone say, "What's wrong with Buda?" That's what they called me. "Nothing is wrong with her. She wants to be with God", said Ricco as he inhaled his cocaine.

The girls were laughing saying. "Let's get naked!"

"That's right, get naked!" I overheard Ricco say loud enough for me to hear. "Tomorrow I'm going to take her to the graveyard and leave her there, then we'll see if God will come get her!"

The girls were laughing "You are God baby!"

That was the moment I began to believe that if there was a God he didn't love me. Five years had passed me by and I was tired of waiting for a God that never came. This was my fifteenth birthday! The party they were having was supposed to be for me. I decided it was time to embrace the game the way the other girls did. It was either that or be left at the graveyard with nowhere to go, left for dead after being brutally beaten. There was no way I was going back to the graveyard. Plus they were getting high and that's what I needed to do. I wiped my tears, got up and closed the door. I put on my makeup and did my hair. Next I put on my diamonds and lingerie. Technically, I had been there the longest and was considered the bottom hoe meaning I would gain favor and have pull if I claimed my position. If I wanted I could take the crown and become his woman and that night I did.

Ricco told me to go out and find other girls if I didn't want to work the streets anymore, so I did. I searched out other girls who were from broken homes, on the streets or just looking to party. I convinced them that they should come with me and have nice things and drive in nice cars. I would transform them from ugly ducklings to beautiful swans. Once they got there, they were not able to leave. I showed them how to work the track and I collected all the money. I bought their clothes and did their makeup. Better them than me.

He started treating me better as my reward. There were thirteen girls all together over the years. Some died by the hands of the johns, and some by the hands of pimps. Some committed suicide and some became addicts to deal with their reality. They were just casualties of the game is what I told myself. I needed to survive. Ricco decided that I was still too young for the track, but old enough to work the club. He knew which ones would accept my fake I.D. I liked it better than the streets and even better than the houses. I had even made some friends there.

Ricco was not having that so he pulled me out. He scheduled me to go back to New York. He actually gave me my ticket. I was surprised; he had never done that in the past. I checked flight schedules. I had a layover so I booked a ticket for Hawaii. I just got on a different flight from what was prepared for me by the madam. I had to pay her back and make some money for myself before Ricco could figure out where I was. The madams thought they were so damned smart. They try to say the johns are clean, this one tried to convince me that they all were her personal boyfriends. I knew she was crazy as hell. She kept asking me who my agent was. She kept finding debt that I still owed to her. Then one morning there was a loud knock on the door, a bang and a scream. I thought it was a police raid. Ricco had entered the building and demanded his money. He had another trigger happy little boy named Tony with him.

He put me in a choke hold and escorted me out of the building. The girl he had with him I knew from the streets. She was not much older than me. It only took him a couple of days to spend my money on dope and women while I watched in disgust. Ricco's mother became sick and he needed to fly home quickly. He cried and said how sorry he was. Then Tony and Ricco flew home. Ricco went back to jail and couldn't get back to us. I stayed in Hawaii, trying to make ends meet. I had no valid I.D., or knew anyone who could make sure I had a place to live. I tried to use our fake I.D. that I got from the check cashing store but most places wouldn't accept it. I was alone and three thousand miles away from home with nowhere to go. I wandered the streets for days stealing food and sleeping in cars. One morning I woke up in a strange man's car. He woke me up saying, "Excuse me ma'am, I have to go to work now." He was very nice about it. I walked around until I found a graveyard. At least it seemed familiar...

~ Four ~

Chaos and Mayhem

I hung out there for a while, screaming out to God, "Why me?" I thought God hated me because he deserted me. I wanted to reach out to my family but I just didn't think they would want me. I didn't think that anyone cared if I was dead or alive. I felt that after everything I had been through, no one would want me. I had no choice but to go back to the block and choose a pimp. I hoped it would be one that wouldn't beat me.

I found another pimp against my better judgment. He was younger than Ricco but His eyes were full of ambition and his smile was comforting. He told me how he needed me. His name was Christian. I never paid any mind to the young girl he was pimping with two black eyes and a broken nose. I was not quite sixteen yet. He was actually nice to me for about a week until one day we were riding with someone else. I was in the back seat of the car, so I smiled at him through the mirror. He accused me of smiling at the other pimp and kicked me in my stomach until it took my breath away.

He continued kicking me on my arms and legs. I could barely move for hours. I would work sixteen to twenty hours a day for the next three years. He would cry after he beat me and buy me teddy bears, jewelry, and clothes every day, trying to even out the pain he had inflicted on me. I was so exhausted from working so hard I would pass out on the track. We lived in Honolulu, Hawaii. He beat me so much that I was black and blue all the time. I wasn't allowed to ever stop moving or socialize or have friends. He always used to say, "Ducks get drunk and talk shit to each other, and about each other, all night." He told me I was a stallion because I was about my money. I wanted to stop, I just didn't know how. I was sure I made a million dollars by now, and tired of being with him, and he knew it.

I saved some money and flew to D.C. There was a killer on the loose. The girls on the track warned me. It went in one ear and out the other. I needed to get money fast.

I started to hustle immediately, not paying attention to where I was going or what I was doing. I as so frightened that I might be noticed and that Christian might catch up with me. He would be looking for me by now. Birds of a feather flock together. I was afraid of one of his pimp friends recognizing me and calling him. I jumped in a car with the first guy who offered me three hundred dollars. I was around seventeen years old at this time. It was a white man in his late thirties. He said he wanted to go to his house. He told me that his house was just twenty minutes away. Thirty minutes went by and we still were driving.

His fists were clenched as I asked him to pull over at the gas station. It was too far to jump out. I thought he was going to try to knock me out so I leaned my body over his hand. That way he couldn't backhand me. He just kept driving. Suddenly, there weren't any lights anywhere. We were in the mountains. I remembered what the girls had said to me earlier. He pulled over and said he had to use the restroom. He attempted to open my door. I saw him come around the car so I locked my side. He got back in on his side of the car and grabbed his keys.

He came back around on my side of the car and attempted to unlock the car door again. This time he said, "You are going to get out of my car now!" I jumped over the driver's seat and out the door. I kicked my shoes off and began to run as fast as I could. I felt my feet opening up as the sharp rocks went into my skin. He chased me saying, "I'm going to kill you bitch!" I ran faster yelling "No you're not!" I felt no more pain. He started his car start and I saw the head lights. I dashed up the mountain and through the trees. The car stopped but I kept running. I broke to the left through more trees. My face, arms, and legs were burning. I didn't stop. Back and forth I weaved my way up the mountain; he had gotten out of the car, so I went back down to the gravel. He got back in the car to try and catch me. He continued to chase me up and down the mountain before he gave up.

It was so dark that I couldn't see anything up in those mountains in the middle of the night. It was complete darkness! The only hint of light was the stars which literally looked as if they were a million miles away! A car finally drove by. I dropped to my knees in the middle of the freeway, threw my hands up in the air, begging for a ride. I was stranded for another twenty minutes, waiting for another car to come by, shaking fiercely and unable to breathe. Finally, another car came by, and luckily, he was a security guard who was working at a nearby psychiatric hospital. He took me to the downtown D.C. police station where they wanted me to stay in town to help find the killer of ten women in that area. I was afraid to stay. I told them I just wanted to leave. The police didn't even ask how old I was. I went back to the track, jumped in a car with two guys for four hundred dollars. On the way back, they pulled out their pistols and demanded their money back. I jumped out of the moving car.

~ Five ~

Living to Die

Needless to say, I jumped on the next flight smoking back to Hawaii and Christian. Things were different. I dreamed of killing him every night. I dreamed of me leaving him again. He continued to abuse me. On my twentieth birthday, I woke him up and begged him to let me go. I told him about my dreams. I told him I wasn't going back out there - not now, not ever. He got up nonchalantly, walked to the end of my bed, and grabbed my feet. Christian dragged me into the living room and tossed me over the balcony. I dangled there wishing he would drop me. I didn't fear for my life or cry. When he pulled me up and beat me until my eyes were bleeding I went into the kitchen and got some ice. Without saying a word I covered my face with make-up and put on my weave. I went to work as usual. He said I didn't have to go, but I would do anything to get away from him at this point. All night long I convinced myself that I was stronger than him.

I paused for a moment, leaning against a streetlight. Suddenly I felt my feet being snatched from under me. I felt my head hitting the ground. I must have passed out. When I came to, it felt like rocks going into my skin. I realized I was being dragged down the middle of the street by Christian. Sadly to say it was on the busiest street in Honolulu. Rage surged thru my body and I pulled the straight razor from my pocket. I opened it with one hand, leapt up with the other hand and grabbed his hair so that he could be closer to me. I sliced his ass from the bottom of his chest to the top. He flagged a cab and I walked away. Later that morning I was still wandering around not knowing what to do or where to go. I looked to the heavens and thought, "Why does God love all the little children but me?" The thought was overwhelming, even for me. A tear started to fall from my face. I didn't even realize I was crying until someone asked me in a very kind voice, "Are you okay?"

I had never heard those words before – in my life. I laughed a little before looking up. When our eyes met I saw something I had never seen. I couldn't put my finger on what it was. She was Hawaiian and black. She was very beautiful. I could tell she was not a working girl. A professional would never be caught dead in flip-flops. I realized that she was an innocent. She was an average young lady around my age who had a family and had just finished high school. We became real good friends. She used her school ID and got me a room. She let me hang out with her family. It was really cool. I'd never had a friend before. I had nothing to offer her back that was worth anything. I started stripping to support myself. We soon found out she was pregnant. Her boyfriend was a military man from the Virgin Islands. It wasn't long after that he asked her to marry him and they moved away to the Virgin Islands. I was glad to see her go and proud to have been her friend. Then I realized I was alone again. I finally got a place of my own.

They let me stay and pay five hundred dollars a week. I thought I was doing well until the loneliness started kicking in. I started drinking again, up to two or three fifths of vodka a day. I had to take acid to withstand the liquor I was consuming and still keep working. I had things to buy you know. Shopping became a fix again. Around this time I heard that my baby brother was on his way to prison, tried as an adult for three counts of attempted murder. I felt responsible for letting him down. I left him there alone with those blood sucking vampires.

It wasn't long before Christian found me. I came home from work one evening, staggering on the elevator. The elevator stopped suddenly. As I turned to my right, I heard a bang. I had just been hit very hard. I felt myself passing out. I was not going to let anyone kill me tonight so I grabbed the wall and pushed myself up. I felt my fingers go inside his eyes. I heard a scream and opened my eyes to Christian screaming like a girl. I pushed the go button and the elevator opened.

Christian ran out the door and out of the apartment building. The next day was work as usual. That night Christian came into the club. He started tearing up dollars and throwing them on the stage. I jumped off the stage and tried to attack him again. He was asked to leave the club. He turned to me and said, “It's not over until I say it's over.” I wasn't scared of him anymore. A couple of days later, while I was working the back room, a tall thin white man walked in. We chatted a while over a bottle of champagne. We arranged to go back to his hotel. After work we caught a cab. On the way there I felt uneasy. When we stepped out of the cab, something told me to leave but I didn't. As soon as we walked into the hotel, I knew my life was over.

There was Christian and three other pimps, all dressed to impress in thousand dollar suits and diamonds on their fingers. There was nowhere to run but I showed no signs of fear. Nodding and laughing, they took me upstairs; I followed without saying a word. There was a table in the middle of the room. They told me to sit down and I did. They sat across the table staring at me. I didn't dare look up. They begin to speak, “Look it here girl, this is the beginning of your new life. Look up and make the right choice.” I stared piercingly and angrily. Even though I was terrified I didn't dare show fear. The man speaking was very dark skinned and super loud. The sound of his voice was so angry and scary. He had a long straight perm in his hair and talked real fast and hard. He offered me a drink then began saying things like “That's my hoe man! She wants to be with this pimping.” I just slid the glass back to him.

The second pimp asked me to take a walk with him. As we walked he told me to notice the pictures, clothes, jewelry, and furniture that all belonged to me. The condo was a replica of the one Christian and I had together. His voice was low and smooth. He was tall and slim, well-mannered and very well groomed. He said things like, "This is all yours. You can have all of it back. I'm not a pimp, I'm a Mac." I just held my head down and shook it as if to say no and that I didn't want it.

The third man had long naturally curly hair that he wore back in a ponytail. He had green eyes and spoke with a lisp. He handed me a three carat ring and said, "You know you're going to die here. Don't you want to live? Come with me to my ranch in Texas. I will keep them from killing you. We can leave right now." I shook my head no to decline his offer as well. They all looked at each other and left the room. I felt the shadow of death pass me by. Steel cold air filled the room and I knew life as I knew it was about to end.

Death was coming and I was ready to die. I would rather be dead than live under these conditions. They came back in the room, and sat a tray in front of me filled with rock cocaine and a big glass pipe. The last thing I heard was Christian whispering in my ear. "If I can't have you, I will make sure no other man will ever want you. Smoke this and I will let you go bitch. You want to be free to live your own life. This is the only way you're going to walk out of here." I didn't know about crack. I had tried powdered cocaine when I was with Ricco. I thought to myself, "This is nothing! I can recover from this." I began to smoke and everything became like a dream.

I didn't care about them assaulting me, raping me or laughing at me. I just kept smoking. They showed me how to rock it and smoke it as much as I could, as fast as I could. I don't remember eating or sleeping at all. I can sometimes still hear them laughing. One day no one showed up, I was too high to move. I stayed there tweaking, looking for pieces of rock and scraping the pipe. Tweaking is just crawling around on the floor looking for remnants of drugs. I must have been there for about three months. I was so weak and out of my mind, I couldn't think of anything but the pipe and the fear. I heard someone say "she's done". They opened the door and told me to get the hell out. I could barely walk. My body was moving against my will. I was starving and I was thirsty but they continued laughing as I walked out the door.

I went back to my apartment and there was a bolt lock on the door. I went to see the manager. His window was open and he was on the phone. I was sure he was calling the police on me. I didn't dare see the police. So I left and went to my job that evening. My boss refused to let me work. He said he couldn't let me work like that, I looked horrible. I hadn't really seen myself yet.

I had some money stashed in a check cashing box that they didn't get. I left my job feeling hungry, weak and terrified. On the way there I ran into a lady who had seen me there before. She told me that they were using my apartment as a crack house and that I probably shouldn't go back there. I thought I just needed to get out of Hawaii and everything would be okay. I used the money to fly to San Diego, California to start again. I got a room and stayed inside long enough to sleep and eat. I needed to build my strength so I could go back to the track before I ran out of money.

It's funny, looking back on it now, I didn't consider myself a crack addict so I had some mental clarity to hide my stash and buy the plane ticket. Mind over matter...

~ Six ~

Crack Head

I found out from a cabby where the track was that the girls worked and geared up. I worked for about a month or so before the pimps started putting it together that I had no pimp. I was on my way to work in a cab and noticed a glass pipe on the seat. I grabbed the pipe, got out of the cab and hit the pipe. I felt obsessed to get more. I went to the liquor store and bought alcohol so I could stop tweaking and start working. I knew I was going to have to choose again soon but I was sure I was not going to choose another pimp. I jumped in a cab about three in the morning and asked the cabby "Do you know where I can get some dope at?" He acted dumb like he didn't know what I was talking about. The urge to continue to get high was overwhelming and it was driving me. I had no control over the desire.

So I told him take me to where the crack heads are. He started to laugh and nodded his head. I spotted a junkie and followed him to the dope man standing on a street corner. I boldly walked up to him with a hundred dollar bill and bought ten rocks. There I was in a red lace dress with a big red ribbon in my strawberry blonde weave down the middle of my back. I followed this junkie into a house full of Crips. I broke the owner of the house off one of my rocks and proceeded to the back room smoking dope. I could hear someone arguing. There was a male voice saying, "Let's rob that hoe!" Next there was some arguing and then there was silence. The lady of the house came into the room and said

"Someone wants to talk to you."

I walked back to the living room and there were some Crips including the one who I bought the dope from. I heard a voice behind him say "Where you from girl?" I told him I was from Hawaii and I just needed somewhere to smoke. He was young, handsome with long curly black hair.

He spoke with a lisp. "Why didn't you buy that dope from me girl?" Realizing that I was in his spot, and that the other guy wanted to rob me, I walked over to him and knelt down in front of him. My face was close to his and I said "If I give you all my money will you take care of me and keep me safe? So I can smoke all the dope I want tonight?" He said "Yes". I reached in my pocket and handed him seven hundred dollars. I told him when I was done smoking I needed a hotel room. He agreed. I went back in the back room and continued what I was doing. When I was ready to go I told him and he got me a hotel room. Everybody called him Scottie Boy.

He was different from any man I had been with in the past. I asked him if he was a Crip. He told me he didn't bang, but that his family does. He said, "I'm just a hustler." I told him "Me too!" We both laughed. He was so handsome and seemed so harmless. He said "How can I be down with you because I need some of that money you getting". I told him to be my man. "I will teach you my hustle."

We became inseparable like Bonnie and Clyde. He introduced me to his family. That was a first! He was always nice to me, I liked that. His family was even nice to me. It was the first time I had ever actually been a part of a family. I wanted to do right and be a good woman for Scottie, but I didn't know how. At first I kept him because of all the money I would make. Soon my drug addiction got in the way. Scottie wasn't a pimp and he soon got bored with the game. He wanted me to stop using and stop hoeing. He wanted me to get a job and be a part of his family. I wasn't ready for that. I didn't have the type of faith and love for myself that he had for me. Scottie hunted me down in and out of crack houses for three years trying to fix me. He was frustrated that getting high was more important than him. One time

Scottie found me in the closet tweaking on the ground, looking for dope. I knew I was hurting him, I could see it on his face. One summer I went to jail. I would go there to build my strength up. Smoking that dope made me weak and out of my mind.

Sometimes I would have to go to jail, just to keep from killing myself or losing my mind completely. I found out that my mother died while I was in jail. I laughed and laughed then I became enraged. I broke a girl's nose and attacked a guard. They sent me to the psyche ward where I would get therapy to help me deal with the death of my mother. I was introduced to Narcotics Anonymous and a psychotherapist. I didn't remember my life before the pipe. I couldn't remember my family, or how I came to be a hoe at this time. The therapist put me in a trance and my childhood years came rushing back. Like a movie playing in my mind; came flashes of incest, flashes of violence - all distorted. It was the worst thing I had ever encountered. I couldn't shut it off. They medicated me to the point I could barely talk. When I got out of jail I went back to Scottie. He took me home to his mother's house. He tried to get me into a program. I hated myself and what was in my mind. I left and continued to get high. Dope was the only thing that turned those cameras off.

My using became more and more obsessive. I never could get high enough to shut it off completely. I never told Scottie why. He thought that he failed me somehow. I knew I had to let him go. I was stopping him from moving on. He wanted out of the game.

He had to keep dope to keep me. Even then it wasn't enough. I told him he had to go on without me. I told him he should find him a square and make a life for himself without me. He wanted no parts of that. I found him other hoes but they weren't what he wanted. Scottie wanted me. Our relationship became very hostile but he never hit me. He just wanted me to change. I went to jail again the following year. The doctors put me back on medication and stuck me back in psyche ward. They tried to reach me. I think they felt a little responsible for the hallucinations I was having. They tried to reconnect me with my family and found my father. He told me he wanted me to come back to Michigan. I missed my family and really wanted to see them.

I went back to Grand Rapids, Michigan to see my family and my father after getting out of jail. When I saw my father he seemed as though he had shrunk. He was eighty-two years old and told me he had learned to write and had stopped drinking. He told me he was in a group called Narcotics Anonymous. He said I should seek them out and let them help me. Then he began to tell me how the white people in my family were devils. He said my mother was the reason all these things happened to me because she was the devil. Meanwhile I was having flashbacks of him molesting my sisters. I wanted him to say he was sorry for hurting my mother and hurting our family. He forbade me from seeing them, because he said they knew what was going on and they didn't care and didn't try to help me. He said he was too weak and too old to take care of himself anymore and that he wasn't strong enough to give himself insulin shots. He needed me to help him. The only thing I could do was run. I asked him for forty dollars and I told him I would be back.

I left his house and went hustling for crack. After about a week of running I walked up to that place called The Island that I knew so well as a young girl. I met an old friend of a friend named Sam. I asked about a hoe that I turned out over ten years ago, he told me she had been stabbed thirty-two times by a high school teacher. I got a paper and went to the local bar. I read about two young girls whose body parts had been found off the highway right outside of the city I was working in. Rumor was, there was a serial killer in town. I drank a couple of shots and went back to the track to hustle up some money. I was coming down hard and the hallucinations were coming back strong. I jumped in an eighteen-wheeler. We drove for about ten minutes then he parked and I jumped in the back. I heard what sounded like a chain. I tried to turn but he overpowered me and handcuffed me. Within seconds he told me to shut up and be still or I would die, then he started driving. He drove for thirty minutes. I started talking to him telling him my name and I asked him if he was going to kill me. He stayed silent; I tried everything to get him to talk and to identify with me as a person. I thought about the girls in the newspaper. I asked him "Did you kill those women and chop them up like that." He said "I might of". I told him I wasn't afraid to die and that I wanted to die. I asked him to kill me quick. I prayed to God that he would take my life quick. I cried silently so he couldn't hear me. Tears were rolling down my face as I asked God to forgive me for my sins and let me die and join Him in heaven.

Suddenly, I felt a peace come over me. The tears stopped and I remained silent. The truck stopped. I felt a click on my wrist. He opened the door and got out of the truck. As I lifted up one of my hands, I became free. I heard the Spirit say "Run or die". I opened the door, jumped out of the truck and ran. I ran right past him on the telephone in a phone booth. I ran through the parking lot, jumped over a rail and ran down the hill to a nearby freeway.

I ran as fast and hard as I could. Didn't look back. I heard gunshots, but I kept running. I heard another shot and ran into the middle of the freeway where there was a center piece and I waited there for the highway patrol. As the state police drove me back to the city, they asked me where I lived. I suddenly remembered my father. They dropped me off at my brother's house. I told him we had to go check on dad. He wanted to wait until the morning. I was frantic and crying that we had to go now. We went to the place of residence where my father lived. They said he was gone. He'd had a stroke while alone in the house. He was at the hospice when we got there, they said there was nothing anyone could do. They said he would die before the night was over. My brother left to find my younger brother. I stayed there with my father, crying and begging him not to leave me. The doctor came in and told me I had to let him go in peace. He suggested to me that I hold his hand and tell him it's okay.

I wasn't ready for him to die. I held his hand. I cried out to him, "Father I love you, please forgive me. I'm sorry daddy, I am so sorry!" I felt his hand tighten around mine as I looked at him. It was as if he was smiling at me, just for a moment. Then it stopped. I thanked him and kissed his head. I laid down in the big chair next to him and fell asleep. The doctor woke me at about 6:30 in the morning and told me "He is leaving us now". I saw my father struggling to hold on to his life. I rubbed his head and said "It's okay daddy, it's okay". His eyes were piercing into mine as he took his last breath. I felt his spirit pass through me and I knew that my father left a piece of him with me that morning.

~ Seven ~

NO WAY OUT

I left and immediately started getting high. I didn't even go to my dad's funeral. My shame and guilt over his death and my mother's death wouldn't allow me too. I hated myself even more for hating them. On the inside I felt like an animal, not even human anymore. I went back to California, it took me three months.

I don't know how I got back there. I was out of my mind. I just recall being in Atlantic City for a while. I stayed so high that I never knew the month or the day. When I got back to California, Scottie had found someone else. I was proud of him for moving on.

I didn't want to live any more. I hated life and the people in it. My world was a cruel, mean place to me where no one cared about each other. I was just ready to go. To heaven or hell it didn't matter. I figured, how much worse could hell be than my current life? So I went to the store and bought three bottles of Tylenol P.M. gel capsules. I mixed them with about $100 worth of heroin and a fifth of vodka, then sat there on the green box on Elcohon Blvd. and Fifty Second St. in San Diego, California. I was laughing; laughing at every one who had tried to hurt me. I was finally going to win. No matter what, nothing or no one would ever hurt me again. Then I saw a dope fiend associate. He asked me what was going on, I told him about what I done. He didn't believe me though.

He said he had a lot of dope and asked me to go home with him. I knew he wanted to take advantage of me because I was high and nodding out. I figured what the hell; I would go out with a bang. He would be having sex with a corpse before the night was through. I made it to his house and must have passed out around six that evening. I woke up around six the next evening. It was like a jolt of energy hit me. I jumped up dizzy, not able to see well and staggered into the bathroom, barely lifting my head. I looked in the mirror, shocked that I was still alive. A closer look and I saw that I didn't have any white in my eyes. My pupils had dilated extremely larger than they ever had before. My skin was green. I felt the shadow of death hovering over me. I stumbled into the living room. The room was full of crack heads smoking dope. They all stopped when they saw me. I looked up and smiled at my friend and told him, "You'd better take me outside because I'm about to die." Then I passed out.

I felt the hard cement against my body. It seems I had been driven to the hospital and thrown from the car in front of the emergency room. I crawled from the ground into the emergency doors.

I lifted my head long enough to look up at a doctor walking by before I passed out again. I heard him screaming, "Oh my God what have you done?" I must have been in a coma or something because I could hear my brother crying. The hospital had contacted my family and told them I was going to die within the hour. I heard my brother saying "Please don't die. Please don't leave me". I asked him why he was crying. He asked me "Are you going to die?" I told him that I was just tired. Then I passed out again. I woke up a few days later, still in the hospital, not dead. I looked around in disgust. I was angry with God for not letting me die. The doctor walked in and told me that I had ruined seventy percent of my liver and I should be dead. He said if a thousand people had done what you have done, one might have lived.

I looked at him and asked "Why? Why, did you save me? I have no place to go! I'm already dead anyway! I don't want to live!

He asked me "Why?"

I told him "I hate this world full of wolves eating me alive, I want to die! I want to die. I don't want to be here, I hate it here".

He walked towards the door and turned to me and said, "We don't let people die like that here. You chose one of the most horrible ways to die".

I couldn't wait to leave the hospital. They kept me under a twenty-four hour suicide watch and then released me. That was a joke, my life was a joke. It was obvious I couldn't take care of myself. Scottie came and got me. He took me to his sister's house. He still loved me. I think I hated him because he could love and I couldn't. He had another girl who loved him. She didn't get high. Yet he still couldn't leave me alone. He stayed with me until I got a little stronger. He wanted me to go searching and get a job. I went and got high. I was gone for days. He told me "I love you Buda but I can't stand to see you like this. You know you're hurting me girl." I started to cry. He said "Now you want to cry. Crying is not going to help you. I tried to help you.

"You know I done everything I could. I'm leaving you! I'm leaving San Diego! I am never coming back. I am not going to stay here and watch you die. All you do is cry!"

He stayed a few more days, got me a hotel and told me it was over. He came to check on me from time to time. He told me to do my thing and use his name so no one would try to hurt me. I couldn't stand being alone. I needed a man that would take care of me and protect me from myself.

It wasn't long before one found me. I was on the elevator going up to my room when on walked a giant. I put my head down quickly as I said hello. Scottie hadn't been around in a couple of weeks and I needed some dope. He wouldn't answer my calls so I got dressed about midnight thinking "I'll show you". I walked down the street a few blocks. As I approached the alley I saw the giant again. Standing there smiling at me, with his hands on his hips like Super Man. I started crossing the street. Then I heard one of my homies call out to me. I had gotten high with him and his girl a couple of times.

He said "What's up Buda?" I told him I needed to get

some shit. He said "Old boy got you."

I was like "Hell no. I am not messing with him." So he got it for me. We got high all night long. I kept sending him back to get the dope. That morning his girl came in and said "Somebody wants to meet you." I was out of money so I went to see who it was. It was the giant in a little sports car. He didn't look so threatening in his car. Then he smiled. The most secure smile I had ever seen. He just nodded and told me to come here. I wasn't quite sure if I should? Then old girl was like "Do you know who that is? Girl, that's Myron."

I looked at her, then looked at him and said "I'm out of here." I ran over and jumped in.

He said, "What's wrong with you?"

I said, "I don't know really! Ugh and I'm not a crack hoe."

He said, "I know that girl. That's why you're in my car. I'm not going to hurt you. I just was checking you out. You're Scotties old girl right?"

"You do your homework don't you?"

"That's my job!"

I laughed.

Then he said, "Yeah, that's what I'm talking about. What's your name?"

I said "Buda!"

He looked at me with a strange look! He said, "You look more like a "Boodles". Then he nodded and said "Yeah, that's what I'm going to call you, Boodles".

I laughed again. "Where are you taking me?"

"To my secret hideout."

I asked him if he had any condoms.

He said "I got two boxes."

By this time I was laughing hysterically. He told me not to worry about nothing, he was going to take good care of me. I was so relieved to hear him say that. I believed him too. He was older and clean cut; he had muscles I didn't even know existed. We went through every one of those condoms that night. I never met a man who had a sex drive like that.

He asked me, "What we going to do about Scottie?"

I said "Who?"

"You know, your man."

I told him it was over between Scottie and me.

He said, "Good, because now you're mine."

Myron became my daddy overnight. He could always make me laugh, even when I wanted to cry! Over the next six months I spent a lot of time with him. Scottie had left California, so I depended on Myron. When I woke up he was there, when I went to sleep he was there. It didn't bother me that he was gone every night. I was twenty-two and he was thirty-four. He was my hero. They called him 'Captain Save a Hoe.' Making love to him was like riding a black stallion at full speed into the midnight sky with fireworks going off all around us! I had found a temporary fix.

He soothed me and allowed me to escape the pain I was in some of the time. I was happy that at last I could feel something other than my own pain. He made me laugh and he made me happy. I didn't care that he took all my money. I didn't have any I.D or social security card. I didn't even exist outside of the jail system. I could barely tell time, let alone take care of myself. He knew that and tried to make sure I had a place to sleep at night. Even still I didn't feel human. I would cut myself and try to overdose daily.

Myron tried to monitor the drugs I used. He would take my money so I couldn't buy dope. He would take me away from the city and the track so I didn't have any way to get money or drugs. Once he was looking for me and I was in the closet hiding, getting high. He wrote in lipstick on the door 'Escape Mechanism!' I hadn't really come to the realization that I had a problem with drugs yet. I thought I got high because I wanted too. Not because I had too. I couldn't go to sleep if he didn't make love to me. He started becoming less and less available.

I was sitting in the room with him one day, he walked out; then came back running! He said "Get off my bed, my wife is coming!" It made me mad but I never said anything about it, other than asking what made her so special? He said; "Ummm she can hold an intelligent conversation. That's why!"

We had been together about a year when I was hanging out with my friend I got high with - Reece. We saw a

Hawaiian looking chick walking up the street. She was beautiful like me. Reece said; "That's Myron's other hoe. That's your new wife in law." We became roommates as well. Her name was Mary and she had been with him for eleven years even before his wife. I really didn't care. I just needed him to do what he did so I wouldn't kill myself. We had a love-hate relationship because he couldn't control me. I did what I wanted too. He didn't like that. He also had another girl who had his baby. We all knew about each other. We would seek each other out just to see what his fascination was with the other.

Sometimes his wife and I would fight. My roommate Mary would always lock me out. She treated me badly, even though I tried to be nice to her. We hated each other and fought a lot. None of them liked me very much. I didn't care. I was never very faithful to him either. He didn't like that so we broke up a lot. We always got back together though. The chase was a lot like getting high. No one really had any control of anything the other one did. This went on for four or five years. He went to the penitentiary twice during that time. The second time things got real hard for me.

My mind was going "it's getting harder to take care of myself". Like the lone wolf I slept in parks during the day, and hustled at night. No name - no face - no resting place. Sometimes I would stand alone by the alley trying to get people to follow me so I could try and kill them or they would kill me. I went from suicidal to homicidal like night and day. One morning I was homicidally out of my mind, waiting for the gas truck to come to the local gas station in my neighborhood. I bought some 151 and made a torch. I just decided to blow up the neighborhood. I told some other junkies that were in the neighborhood what I had planned. They must have believed me. They gave me a hit and stole my lighter. When the gas truck came and the man driving it opened the hole in the ground. I walked up to him, with my bottle of 151 rum. I had my torch hanging from it. I looked in his eyes and I said "Are you ready?" He looked at me discouraged and confused. When I removed the bottle from my jacket, his eye's widened and he said "Please!" Then I realized that my homies stole my lighter.

I started laughing and walked away to find them. They were hanging out in this garage down the alley. They started laughing when they saw me. "You really need some sleep girl!" I didn't want to sleep I wanted to kill someone. They said they were going to get some dope and locked me in that garage. I finally went to sleep for what must have been three days. I woke up with people all around, moving fast and talking fast. I was so weak and so tired.

One of the homies bought me some food and gave me a hit. I was off and running! I could get some dope to wake me up. I would have such terrible hallucinations, of people screaming and children crying; constantly day and night. I would feel things touching me, even when no one was there. I started attacking the tricks that tried to take advantage of me because I was high. One guy was really big and he tried to overpower me and take his money back. I got out the car and started to run.

I fell and hit the ground. My hand landed on a huge brick. The brick was much bigger than my hand. I felt him running up behind me. I turned and he moved in to attack me. I hit him! I hit him with the brick in his face as hard as I could. I saw blood pouring out of his right eye. A few days later an older white man picked me up. I thought 'this is going to be quick, easy and safe.' As I got in his truck I noticed a rug cutter in the middle of the seat. As soon as the car stopped he grabbed my left arm. He said "You're going to do what I tell you or else you're going to lose this!" I reached over with my right arm, grabbed the open blade and opened him up from his wrist to his forearm. I went to jail. He told the police I robbed him. That was lie! I asked the police to check his wallet. If I robbed him then why did he have money and I didn't. I knew the law. I told the police that he was assaulting me. I told them he was trying to rape me! I demanded that they charge him also. The police knew me as well. They practically watched me grow up. They charged him with assault and attempted rape. He dropped the charges. My case was dismissed and I was released the next day.

Things were getting out of control. I had seen a story

about a woman they called the Monster. She was a hooker who started killing her customers. I could relate to the hate. I was scared of turning into that type of monster. I had never hurt anyone, other than to just get away from them hurting me. Things where escalating. I felt it within me. A couple days later, I got in a fight with some dark-skinned girl from out of town trying to make a name for herself. She thought I was white and weak. She started talking loud. I wasn't tripping until she swung at me, that was all it took. I broke her nose against the cement and drug her face against the street; stomping her and kicking her. I would have killed her if it wasn't for my friend watching the fight. I knew I needed help. I couldn't contain the rage within me any longer. I couldn't be around people for fear I might hurt them. I couldn't be alone either for fear I would hurt myself.

I started snorting heroine to slow my thoughts down. I wandered around sometimes not even knowing my own name, or what city I was in. I just was. I didn't care anymore. I woke up one day in a field. There where bugs crawling on me and in my hair. I started screaming trying to get them off me. I fell to my knees and I asked God "Why won't you let me die? How am I supposed to live this way?" Then I remembered that if there was a God, He didn't care about me. I reached in my pocket to find a crack rock, some heroine, and a twenty-dollar bill.

I looked up to the heavens and said "thank you!" Then I put the rock on my pipe and took a hit. Sniffed some heroine and walked up the street to the local bar. I saw a police car parked at the corner doing paper work. I went in the bar where I had a couple shots of hard liquor. Walking back outside I got in the back of the police car. The officer said. "What do you want?

I said "I got thirty thousand dollars' worth of warrants. Take me to jail I'm tired."

He said "It is Christmas Eve! My wife just finished dinner and I'm off duty."

I begged him; "Please I'm tired! I have nowhere to go!"

He said "I don't care! Get out of my car! You stink!"

I pulled out my pipe and took a huge hit. He turned and

said “Hey you can’t do that in here!”

Before he finished the sentence I exhaled in his face. He was really upset, cussing and yelling at me. He handcuffed me and took me downtown. I was happy. I was tired. I did six months in jail before even seeing a lawyer. I was wild and mean, even started gang wars. I snatched people off the bunks in the middle of the night and beat them down.

I hated people so much! They took me out of population and put me with a lifer called Nickbottom. She was famous for causing chaos in jail. Even the guards approached her with caution. We got along great. They kept us heavily sedated on Thorazine so we wouldn’t be a harm to ourselves or anyone else. I told Nickbottom about how much I wanted to hurt people.

I told her about what I had been doing to the girls up in there. She looked at me and said “Yeah, you remind me of me. I'm going to spend the rest of my natural life in prison. I'll be holding it down when you get there. Don’t worry about nothing they got a cell just for you too, if that’s what you want. Then I’ll see you when you get there.”

She laughed and fell into a nod. That was the first time I felt anything in a long time. I knew she was right. My life flashed before my eyes. I knew I would see her again. I cried for the first time in a long time. Even though she was a Blood and I was Crip affiliated, we got along fine.

One morning about four o’clock the guards called me out to go to court. A young white lawyer approached me with enthusiasm.

“Hello Miss Jay you’re going home today. I got you out on time served with three years on probation and a six-year lid”. In other words the court was releasing me with nowhere to go and no means to survive. Three years’ probation; stipulation being if I got in any trouble I would do six years minimum.

~ Eight ~

Trying to Recover

I started thinking about my oldest and youngest brothers. Together they had spent forty years in prison. I started thinking of my dad and my brother who had fought in wars, defending this country. Neither of them had gained much other than shellshock, nightmares, and drug addiction. They hardly had enough income to survive on. I knew if I took this deal I would be signing my life away. I couldn't let all they had been through and suffered through, go in vain. I looked at the young man and said, "You woke me up for this shit. I'm not agreeing to that, you can kiss my ass".

He looked at me all discouraged and asked "Don't you want to go home?

I told him "I have no home. So if you are going to send me to the penitentiary then you can send me now, or I'm not going anywhere."

He turned and walked away. A few minutes later the guard came to take me into the courtroom. I stood in front of the judge. He said "It is my understanding that you don't want to take the offer given to you."

I said "That offer is bullshit your honor. I have nowhere to go, no money, how am I going to live?"

He said, "Well Miss Jay, you have served your time. I can't just send you back to jail."

I felt three generations of rage coming over me. I'm sure my face was red. The temperature went up about ten degrees. I started yelling at the judge. I said, "I been out on these streets since I was ten years old. Been hustled and sold like a piece of meat. No one has ever tried to help me. I'm not going back out there to them wolves. So you can send me to the pen now, Sir."

The judge looked at me. I was hyperventilating and crying, staring back at him in desperation. He said to me "Miss Jay I'm going to let you go back to jail while I review your files. Then I will have a solution for you when you come back".

I was escorted back to jail, back to my cell, back to Nickbottom. I told her what I done. She said it was the smartest thing I would probably ever do. She said "You just might have saved your life." There was a silence between us over the next thirty days. I guess there wasn't much left to talk about.

The guard came to take me back to court. She was a young Spanish girl. I could tell she was a military brat by her persona. She handcuffed me and shackled me. Then she started yelling at me. "Walk against the wall inmate!" She was trying to appear hard-core. I could tell she was a rookie. She pushed me up against the wall. "Who do you think you are? We have been wasting taxpayer's money on your half-breed ass." I just looked at her. Then she said "What war have you been in? What have you done for this country?" I remained silent. I knew she would never understand about the wars I walked through. I knew she came from a sheltered environment where they were taught that in America we all have the same opportunities. She was wrong, and I didn't feel it was my job to teach her. I went back to court.

The judge sentenced me to a year at a place called the House of Metamorphosis. This program was about behavior modification. I went into this with the hopes of something different, something better. The first day at the program I met with the head counselor. His name was Mr. Gibson. I clicked with him. He reminded me of someone in my past. I could tell he had been a hustler like me. I wanted him to be my counselor. He said "I could help you better if I'm not. You need a female counselor." He said I needed to build relationships with strong women. I didn't agree with that. I always thought of women as weak and expendable. Surely didn't think one could counsel me. Plus I was whore and women hated whores. He paired me up with a white lady. Her name was Miss Peggy. I couldn't even bring myself to speak to her. She reminded me of my mother. I soon found out that I was prejudiced.

She appeared to be cold and mean. She turned out to be the exact opposite. Miss Peggy was very understanding and smart. I couldn't get anything past her. She could read me like a book. The first nine months I spent mourning. I mourned for myself, my mother, my father and my family. I had lost so much. I had no friends, no family and was envious and jealous of those who had that kind of support. I was mean and cruel to all the sisters in the program. I wanted to get clean so I could start hustling again. This wasn't for me. I thought I was meant to be a whore. Why else would God have given me this life? Who else could go up against the pedophiles and perverts in America? Why else would God have allowed these things to happen to me? I thought we all had a job to do in life and mine was to make room for those who would die otherwise. It was the only thing that made sense to me.

I got a new counselor because Miss Peggy became ill. There was another counselor named Mr. Walker who assured me everything I had been taught in my whole life was a lie. This made me so angry. He also told me that even I could change. I didn't believe him. He was an L seven square (which meant he had never been to jail or in trouble and was probably raised in the church, a two family home) as far as I was concerned. He had absolutely nothing to give me.

I continued to get into trouble; yelling, screaming and crying all the time. Mr. Walker was always calm. He allowed me to come up with solutions to my own problems. I hated that. He told me I was smart. I laughed, I didn't believe that either. Mr. Walker taught me so much about myself and the world around me. He would argue scenarios with me until I came up with the best solutions for myself. Mr. Gibson, the head counselor kept me motivated by telling me one day I was going to help a lot of people. He told me I would be a good counselor if only I would stop feeling sorry for myself. No one there really wanted to deal with my past much. Now I understand why, looking back on things. I just couldn't handle it all at one time. I still had not surrendered anything even after nine months. I didn't think I could change or even knew if I really wanted too. I blamed everyone and everything for my life. I had been let down by everyone I had ever trusted. I was wild and untamed.

I couldn't even hold a conversation. I would hyperventilate and start stuttering and crying every time I tried. I was in physical pain all the time. I went to the doctor so much that one time he told me I was causing myself to be in pain - mentally. Back at the rehab program, the director was a beautiful, light-skinned black woman. I respected and loved her because her outside matched her insides. I knew that was real power and I wanted to be like that. It was just hard for me to believe that I could. She had seen me struggling and suggested that I write down my feelings. She even went into her closet and gave me some of her suits she didn't wear any more.

That was the nicest thing anyone had ever done for me. That act of kindness changed me inside that day. I felt like she cared about me. Then she got me a job working with a caterer. I was still going back to the old neighborhood. I would hustle every chance I got. It felt good to be able to hustle again for money instead of dope.

One day I just decided that I would rather be high than live with all the physical and emotional pain I was going through. I couldn't look in the mirror without seeing an ugly, hideous monster. Whenever I was alone I would think about people I knew who had died.

I couldn't even eat. I would see acts of molestation and incest and I hated being clean. I still hated being alive and I hated life. I couldn't handle the shame, guilt and all the feelings that came along with being clean. Two weeks before graduation I went out and got high. It felt so damn good when I inhaled, until I exhaled. Then the chase was on. Not eating, not sleeping, having sex for drugs. I quickly became suicidal and homicidal again. It would be two weeks before I even realized what I had done. I stayed out there for three months. Eventually I realized there was nothing left for me out there on the streets. It wasn't long before I was just wandering around not knowing who I was or where I was going; again. I knew I had to go back to the rehab program. One day I just got on the bus and went back.

I sat there at the front door, tweaking out of my mind. I hadn't slept or ate in a week. I sat there for three hours before anyone would see me. Mr. Walker came out and sat across from me.

He asked me, "What are you doing here?"

I said "I want to come back."

He asked "Why?"

"Because I'm dying out there."

"I can see that! You should have gone to detox first."

"I don't need to detox," I said. Then Mr. Walker calmly told me that I was too high to program. (Programs have a daily routine that you have to follow. Most want you to detox for 72 hrs. before they accept you.) He said I needed to come down first. A tear fell down my face and I began shaking my head no with the most serious face, speaking softly. I could make it, I begged him "Please don't make me leave, I don't need to detox I'll be fine."

He went upstairs and I knew I was going to have to deal with Miss Monroe. She was the closest thing I had to a mother. She is still the only woman who I feel that fits that title. She finally called me into her office and asked me why I wanted to come back? I told her I just needed another chance to try and make it. She agreed to let me back inside after I committed to seventeen more months.

I committed to doing everything differently this time around. I began writing down my feelings. I tried to be nicer and more polite to my sisters in the program. They didn't accept me though. I had pissed off a lot of people. Rumor was that I couldn't do it anyway. I stayed clean over the next year or so just because my peers didn't think I could. This time I was paired up with Miss Ross an educated, bougie, light-skinned black lady.

I didn't like her at first. She appeared to be a silver spoon brat to me. She soon showed me that it doesn't matter where you're from or what you've been through. What mattered is how you saw yourself. How you treated the people in your life, and how you treated yourself. She helped me to stop being prejudiced and envious by having me pair up with people who had been raised differently than I had. She had me give people sincere compliments daily so I could see how other people reacted to me being nice to them. Doing that helped me to see people as individuals.

She told me I should take people's feelings into consideration before speaking and decide if what I was about to say or do would offend me. If it would, then I should rephrase it or just not say it. She showed me how to be assertive, not mean and vicious. She taught me how to enjoy my own company by having me go out to the mall and have dinner by myself. I soon learned that I was good company.

I was still hustling though. I needed money or so I thought. One day I was on a day out from my program. I went to the track to hustle as usual. I was standing there in my hoochie shorts and my weave. A customer pulled up and waved for me to come. I walked to the car. At least part of me did. You see I had an out of body experience that day. I watched my self, prancing around leaning in to talk to this complete stranger and I couldn't believe my eyes. I never knew how trifling and disgusting it looked for a woman to exploit herself for money or drugs! For the first time in my life I felt shame. I felt so degraded and humiliated.

In that moment I knew that I couldn't do it. Not then, not ever again. I went back to my program feeling sick inside, felt so dirty. Taking a shower couldn't get it off me. I couldn't hold my head up, couldn't look anyone in the face. I knew I had to tell someone but just couldn't. There was a girl who called me on it in our group session later that evening. She asked me if I was high in front of Miss Monroe, Miss Ross, and Miss Peggy! I tried to explain what I had been doing on my passes. Miss Monroe was furious with me, she told me not only had I disgraced myself; I had disgraced the program. She said "Get your ass downstairs in the exit chair, you disgust me." I don't think I had ever really felt sorry about anything before that day. That was the day that I realized I was sorry! So sorry about everything! I realized all the things I had done. To my mother, to my father, to my family, to my friends - I had betrayed everyone who had ever trusted me. I was just like everyone else who had hurt me in past.

I realized that for the last eight years it was me exploiting me and degrading me. They asked me to rejoin the circle. I had no words; I didn't need to. Miss Monroe knew what to do. She took everything that I had gained from the program; all my hooker clothes, my passes. She had me write notes directly to her for things I needed, even toothpaste. During that time I worked harder than I had ever worked on anything. Mr. Walker suggested I take a long look at my life by writing my autobiography.

He wanted me to focus on my behavior, the choices I made, and the things I was accountable for. It was time I stopped blaming everyone else for my life. He explained to me that I was now a grownup who knew the difference between right and wrong. I was responsible for my actions and my future. He said if I wanted to have a better life then I would have to make better choices, by using common sense and not acting out irrationally. Mr. Gibson told me that I was valuable. He said I should never want to be around those types of men who had hurt me in the past?

He said I should be insulted by their very presence and that I deserved a man who would work for my attention; a man who would find me smart and brilliant. One that would want to marry me. Not for money, not for sex, not as a trophy piece, but just because I was Alice. I became determined to raise me into the woman I would want my daughter to be.

I had to change the way I saw myself fit in my own world. I had to learn to think outside the box. I had to broaden my circles and see past what was right in front of me by setting goals and coming up with a plan that was reachable and achievable. I had to become willing to do something different despite my fears of inadequacy.

I wrote letters to my mother and my predators to try and get some closure so I could move on.

Dear Mother,

I am sorry for the pain I caused you as a young girl. I was angry because you weren't there for me. I didn't feel safe in the house with you so I went out to the streets. I laughed and I was glad when you died. Hate, anger, rage, guilt, shame and degradation consumed my thoughts of you for so long. So many times in my life I wondered why I wasn't good enough for you to love. I am always wondering why you abandoned me and never had a safe place for me to come home too. I was your daughter; I wonder if you knew how much I needed you. I was alone and hungry for love. I had nowhere to go, there was no one there to care for me or guide me. I spent my life hating you and thinking that you hated me too. I surrender my pain today. I surrender my hate today, I surrender you today. I want to be free and I want you to be free. Free from the bondage and the burdens of the past. I know you loved me and you know I loved you too. I am sorry I wasn't there when you died of leukemia. I know it must have been hard for you and painful. I now know you needed me like I needed you. Know that your daughter is safe now and doing much better in life. You can rest in peace now mommy, I'm okay. Good-bye for now. I'll see you soon, but not soon!

Love,
Alice, your daughter

Dear perpetrators,

This letter is to the men who stole my innocence, the men who tortured and raped me. To the men who fed me crack hoping that it would ruin me. You sought me out as a young child, you snatched away my hopes and dreams. You altered my world and destroyed my life. What you have taken from me I can never get back. You hurt me maliciously, then bought and sold me like a slave. You kept me in bondage for your own personal gain or thrill. I was not a human being to you. I come to you now as a woman. I come to tell you that I was a child who deserved a life of hope and opportunity. There is no payment, no pay back or no amount of justice that could restore the pain you caused me. That could mend my heart or restore my spirit. So your apologies are not wanted or necessary. This letter is to inform you that I release any binds you have over my life. I am no longer a defenseless child. I am a survivor of the fittest. Only I can release me, only God can restore me. I have endured all that you had to give and I am still standing.

Alice, former slave
God's daughter

~ Nine ~

Post-Traumatic Stress Disorder

After sixteen months I was feeling good, looking good and ready to go out on my own. I had a secret though, no one knew. I was in a relationship. I had met a man in recovery with three more year's clean time than I had. He was a secret because he worked in recovery. He worked for one of the sister programs. During the course of my program it was suggested that I go to a job readiness program. I'd never had a job before. This place would show me how to apply for a job. That's where we met. We knew it was against the policy. It started out that I would hang out with him on my passes. He was the only person I knew outside of my program who didn't get high. I spent all my free time with him.

I graduated my program and got employed. He was intelligent, handsome and a good lover. He had a car, a job, his own bank account and even went to church. I thought I had done my homework and would finally be a married woman. But he was no different than the other men in my life who manipulated, lied and cheated to get what they wanted. Most of the men I was with in the past were self-centered and arrogant womanizers. They only saw what they wanted and nothing else. Something about that drew me to them. Once I left my treatment program, other things came into the light. I found out he had a lot of other women. I also found out he had a serious gambling habit. But by then I was pregnant! Our story begins and ends with my son who I love very much! He has brought me unspeakable joy. He is a wonderful teacher and keeps hope alive in my world.

My son has taught me about unconditional love and selflessness. Over the next couple years I struggled with homelessness and poverty. I had never been a mother before so I decided that I needed another program, a program that would teach me about being a parent. I checked into a women and children's drug rehabilitation program and stayed there nine months. I took parenting and anger management classes. I don't know if I learned a lot about being a parent, but I surely learned a lot about what not to do as a parent. When my son was almost a year old I started having nightmares about molestation. Being scared and confused about why I was having these dreams, I searched out the therapist to help me work through these times.

I didn't want to change my son, bath him, or dress him. I felt that I might hurt him in some way or that I was not worthy of him. The therapist assured me that I was a kind, loving mother. She assured me that children who were victims of incest or molestation go through feelings of inadequacy. The dreams were just a reflection of my past experiences.

I felt better talking to her about my dreams. I knew that I would never hurt my son and that I was not being hurt anymore. I knew that I was a good parent, having sacrificed my freedom just to learn better ways to parent him. He was definitely worth it. I was determined to give him a life worth living. So, I got a job working on the shipyard, left my program and got a roommate.

Making minimum wage, I still couldn't afford my own place. I didn't like having a roommate. It worked on my behavior so much. To see other people and their character defects was one thing, but living with a person and their flaws was something totally different. You never really know a person until you live with them for a while. Then their true colors start to come out. I kept forgetting things on my job. I also kept loosing important things. I would lose identification cards, money and insurance cards. You know; all the important stuff. I had a hard time focusing on what I was supposed to do on my job, seems I was preoccupied. I couldn't concentrate on my work.

There were just too many men around me. I realized that I was desperate and lonely for male company. I started taking numbers and making dates. It started out as simple fun. I would go on a lot of dates just to pass the time away. I didn't want to chance having another unwanted relationship, so I never got serious with anyone. Over a matter of weeks I realized that I was becoming selfish, manipulative, and using men according to what they had to offer me.

I was still working both sides of the fence, still caught up between the passions of a new life in recovery vs the thrill of the game, and the ties of bondage! There was only one solution. Quit. So I did. My dignity and reputation meant a lot to me and I didn't want to jeopardize the work I had done. Without a job I knew I would have to find somewhere else for my son and me to live.

I really missed my family. I had not seen any of them since I had been clean, or since my dad's death. So I called my nephew and asked him if there was anywhere for us to stay. He said "Yes come on."

He lived with his mom, one of my sisters. She thought I should come too. So I did, against the better judgment of my friends in recovery. I knew that it was time for me to face my past. It was time for me to build relationships with my family members. I knew it was an essential part of my healing process. I packed up my things, headed back to Michigan and moved in with my nephew and my sister. I missed them very much. I wanted so badly for things to work out and tried to be a role model and emulate change. There was a lot of tension in the house. They drank and partied a lot, something I hadn't done in years. In recovery we abstain from alcohol. One drug is no different from the other. I soon found that I was in an emotional and spiritual war. My family members did not have recovery. I felt more alone than I had felt in a long time. Being there reminded me of all the reasons I left home in the first place. Things just didn't work out. My money ran out again and I was about to be homeless with my two-year-old son. I wanted a better life for him.

I needed to find someone to help me care for him. So, I got into a relationship as a desperate attempt to better our life. I felt that since I had been a prostitute for so long, I could make a sacrifice for my son. There was a close friend of the family who had a job and was financially stable. And, he liked me. At first I hesitated getting involved with him. Then things got worse between my family and me and I felt like a complete stranger. I felt like when I walked into the room - they all stopped talking.

We would get into heated conversations about my past. I knew they felt bad about what happened to me. I knew they wanted to help me, realizing that we all had our own demons and our own drama. The more I tried to comfort them the harder it got for me. Winter was here and I had to move on. I knew they felt it too. Everybody decided to go their own way. The only thing about that was, there was nowhere to go and I didn't want a relationship.

'Heavy' was a friend of the family who was nice to me and kind to my son. I pretended too, thinking to myself that lots of women settle to be comfortable, why can't I? We started hanging out at the club, drinking. I got into a relationship with him against my better judgment. He drank a lot and I started drinking with him and I was in recovery.

I got a job working in a shelter for women and children. I had a nice car; my son had his own room. I thought I was living the dream. The thing about dreams is they are just dreams, not reality. In reality, I cried every time he touched me. I couldn't stand to be in the same room with him. There was something very wrong about what was happening. Before long I stopped letting him touch me. I couldn't even sleep in the same bed with him. I gained seventy pounds because of depression about the relationship. I couldn't stand being around him because I felt he robbed me of my clean time. He said he understood and it was okay. I knew it wasn't. I knew I had to leave him. It was just so comfortable not worrying about where my son would sleep. Or how I would feed and clothe him. I started saving money so I could make my move. I loved my job, loved helping other women.

It was the only thing that was real in my life at that time. Once I was called into work unexpectedly, for the overnight shift. But, I never really allowed him to interact much with my son.

I tried to call my baby sitter, but there wasn't enough forewarning and they weren't available. I fed him, bathed him and put him on the couch to watch a movie. I said, "Heavy, just let him watch his movie. I'll get him when I get home." I got about three miles away and suddenly realized I left my laptop. So I went back home. I put the key in the door and turned the knob. To my surprise, Heavy was kneeling in front of my son's mid-section, holding a blanket over him. When I walked in he gave me a funny look, then he jumped up. I was confused.

Then my son said, "Mommy, he is taking my clothes off."

I asked my son "What"?

My son replied sternly "I said, he is taking my clothes off."

Heavy started moving fast, asking him if he wanted his toys and asking him if he wanted another blanket. I asked him what he was doing. He said he was just talking to him. I knew that my presence had startled him. I knew he would be safe for the night. I didn't want to make a scene and then leave. I went back to work, scared and confused.

I called my nephew who lived in the same apartment building and told him what happened. I asked him to go visit Heavy and just hang out until my son was asleep. I resigned from my job the following day. Heavy was training to drive semi-trucks. He left the next day to go to training. I sold my car, emptied my bank account and jumped on a plane back to California. I was appalled and so hurt, blaming myself. I felt that was the price I paid for thinking I could prostitute myself in any form. When you go into something that's bad, it ends up worse. That's just the karma of life. I could see how women sweep things under the rug or just overlook them. I was not confused about what I saw. My son spoke clearly and very plain. I had no other choice, as a mother with understanding and knowledge of molestation, than to react and protect my child. There was nothing that anyone could have told me to make me think differently. Why would my son say someone was taking his clothes off?

At two years old, he didn't understand the dynamics of our relationship. He only understood what mommy told him. No one is supposed to take his clothes off. I felt in my heart that he wanted to hurt my son to hurt me. As a parent it is our responsibility to teach our children what is right and wrong. I was proud of my son. He showed me that all the work I had done was paying off. That he understood and could comprehend, even at age two, what mommy was teaching.

I got back to California; staying with this friend and that friend. I wanted to get a job and start fresh. However, things were different for me. I was very afraid all the time and began having visual hallucinations. I would be walking down the street and someone would be approaching me, no one in particular who was of any real threat. My mind would start playing films of them attacking me. By the time they reached me I would be frozen with fear. Sometimes I couldn't even breathe. Then it just kept getting worse. I tried to ignore what I was thinking.

The hallucinations would override my thinking patterns. I was again becoming defenseless against my thoughts. It wasn't long before, in my mind, I started killing complete strangers, over and over - all day long. I was scared and freaked out. I started thinking about the actual reality of me hurting someone. Being a skilled fighter, I had caused grave bodily harm to other people in the past. So, I stopped going outside by myself. Then I just stopped going out.

Things didn't get any better. I found myself having to go outside, I had to live! When I was alone, I was scared of my own shadow. Whenever I saw it I became frozen with fear, unable to breath. The fact was I didn't feel safe outside or inside or anywhere. Everywhere I went, I felt as though I was on some type of battlefield. The more I resisted, the stronger it got. When I started trying to resist it, I would go into a comatose state. I would shake and have convulsions like I was having a seizure. In actuality, I was going backwards in time. My mind would take me back to the time I had been taken hostage, when I was being tortured, when I was being raped over and over! I would cry out to God to make it stop. A lot of the time I noticed that it helped. I saw my life flashing before my eyes. It was too much, even for me. My son could see my fear. He kept asking me if I was alright. I noticed that he was becoming fearful as well. This was bigger than me and I knew I needed help. I needed to figure out why this was happening. I was ready to commit myself into the hospital. The county mental health hospital immediately medicated me. I hated taking medicine. They set me up with an appointment at a local clinic, the UCSD Psychiatric Outpatient Hospital in San Diego, California.

I knew there was something very dangerous about dealing with this type of psychosis and paranoia at the same time. I went in for a meeting that was supposed to last an hour. It lasted five hours. They put me in front of a panel of fourteen doctors and asked me what was stopping me from killing anyone!

I told them I had a God of my understanding who doesn't allow me to kill anyone for any reason. I assured them that I was there because I didn't want to hurt anyone. I wanted my life back, I wanted my mind back. I needed some time to figure out what was going on with me. I also needed to educate myself about my illness, as well as a safe environment for my son and me, while I learned to develop the skills to arrest it. They gave me a list of numbers to local shelters, then teamed me up with a psychologist and a therapist. They changed my medication and told me I had a mental illness.

They said it was the same symptoms as the men and women who had served in wars. I was suffering from shell shock? The doctors called it severe Post Traumatic Stress Disorder or PTSD. I recognized the disease because my father had it. They said due to the trauma I had suffered as a child and through young adulthood, I would need to be medicated and supervised by a doctor. They wanted to know if there was anyone who could care for my son.

I asked them how long it was going to take. They said there is no assurance that I would ever recover. Most people who had survived the amount of trauma I had, don't ever completely recover. They said they would give me time to find a safe place for my son and me to live, suggesting that I take classes if I wanted to understand the illness. The therapist suggested that I meet with them twice a week. When I left there I was heartbroken. I knew I had to comply, for my own safety and the safety of my son. I knew that it was going to take more than those doctors to help me through this one. I was going to have to consult with the - I AM - the big guy, the one who created the heavens and earth. I knew that if these doctors were going to be able to help me they were going to need help and guidance.

I sat down on the carpet. I inhaled and exhaled, listening to the breeze. I started thinking about my life, again. Tears began to fall. I prayed *"Lord God; father in heaven hear my voice. It is your humble servant Alice; I come to you in pain and agony. My life is in shambles again. Please send your precious son Jesus and the Holy Spirit to counsel with me and console me in my time of need. What would you have me do oh God! I need your help! Please speak to my soul!"* I started to envision myself, walking along a path surrounded by huge trees in the fall. I felt wet leaves on my bare feet. I walked into the springtime, deep in a meadow of flowers and saw a great light coming from the sky. As I knelt there in silence; a spirit came down as a light on the left of me. A man came down to the right of me in all white, with no face. I kept silent and still. Next I saw myself at a river being baptized and anointed with oil. I heard a voice say "Come into my house so you can know me! I have delivered you from bondage why are you still there?

I rode on the wings of an angel soaring through the sky. Once the meditation was over I was back to my reality. Unable to care for my son or myself any longer, I thought maybe God wanted me to go to church. I was willing to do anything at this point. I talked with one my friends in recovery who had a good solid religious relationship with a church. I tried to explain what I was going through.

She spoke to her pastor about me. I went to church for prayer. The pastor wanted to pray over me. She pointed me out in church, then her and a group of women took me in the other room, encircled me and began praying. I was very uneasy because I had not been to church in years. It started out very nice and innocent. They had this look as if they were going into battle. I wasn't sure with who though. They moved in closer and locked me in the circle; praying louder. After speaking in tongues, the pastor said she could see I was being tormented by demons. I felt a great sense of fear.

When she touched me I must have blacked out momentarily and hit the floor. I felt so hot as if I couldn't breathe. I tried to get up but the other women held me down. The pastor said "Grab the holy water, grab the oil!" She started screaming "Come out Demon! Come out!" She began to plead the blood of Jesus to take command over my spirit. She began to call demons by name such as lust, fear, confusion and death. I was shaking fiercely and every time they sprinkled me with the water, I begin to scream out. Every time the women with the oil touched me, I felt pain. I did indeed see demons.

It was as if the demons where standing in front of them or beside them, helping them hold me down. They were saying the same exact things and were laughing and throwing that holy water at me. They prayed over me for about two hours. I am not sure if the pastor was satisfied but I never went back. Just like I didn't see her during that process, I don't believe she could see me either. You cannot help someone you cannot see. I could tell when she looked at me; all she saw was a demon. I knew I wasn't one.

I learned there is a difference between tormenting and possession and that you have to see the good in someone in order to help them. I couldn't deny that there was something there not of God. Something that hated God and hated me! I felt as if I was in a great struggle, full of confusion and fear. Most of all I felt hate deep down inside me. I don't even think the pastor was satisfied that I had been delivered.

Things did get quieter in my head, long enough for me to get a moment of clarity to figure out my next move. I didn't believe that I was some type of demon. Nor did I believe I was mentally ill. One thing was for certain, prayer couldn't hurt.

I loved God for saving my life. I loved God for giving me new life. I believed in God. I knew that the devil and evil was a real thing and I knew it in ways other people just read about. I just wasn't positively sure that God loved me. I was angry with God for having to go through this. After all, I thought I was doing His will. I did change my life. I was working with other women, trying to be a role model and leader in the community. I couldn't figure out what more he wanted from me. I wasn't sure I was even going to make it through this. Definitely couldn't do it alone any longer. My friends understood addiction. They didn't understand mental illness. I couldn't talk to anyone about what was going on.

All they knew is, one day I was accepting life, living life, being a parent. Then one day, I just couldn't. I was tripping out, not able go outside anymore. Hearing things, afraid of my own shadow; even the people closest to me were at a loss as to how to help me. The saddest part was, I didn't know how to help myself. I started calling shelters, trying to find the nicest one that could assist me through this. I needed to be under surveillance and supervised so I could keep my son with me.

I found the San Diego Rescue Mission a residential Christian shelter for women and children. They catered to people suffering from addiction and mental illness. I would meet with a Christian therapist once a week. I got settled in and started going to work. I did my classes and therapy twice a week at UCSD hospital. At this program we studied the bible sixteen times a week. God was the solution for everything. I found that studying the bible gave me an inside look on who created me and why. It is an excellent resource when trying to gain understanding of life itself and the order of things.

People of biblical times suffered a lot. The bible talks about a man called Christ, who is God; then separated from himself in spirit and came to earth in the flesh. He came to earth as the light of the world. He came to the world so that we may live. The world was full of sin and God was going to destroy it. Yet he loved the human race so much he decided to give us the chance to change. So he came down in the form of a man. He was persecuted, beaten and betrayed by someone who was close to him. He lost a friend to death and was faced with temptation. Then he was brutally murdered. He did all this; just so people could be forgiven and not perish but have everlasting life. The bible helped me to understand that there was a reason for suffering. It also showed me that in order to be a good teacher I had to be a good student. I had to stay open to what I was reading and receiving. I was still so angry about what was happening to me, I blamed God. I noticed that in Jesus' time on the earth there were five women of significance. They were all considered unclean or the harlots of their times. It gave me comfort to see how Jesus always came to their defense and gave their life meaning.

Practically on the edge of existence; I needed someone stronger than me to intercede. I learned that God is all-powerful and His power lived within me. The strength I needed to overcome was through Christ, through his crucifixion He had already interceded for me. Meaning, I had already been delivered from my sins and all I had to do was believe that I was. There was a divine reasoning for my suffering and God has a master plan for everyone; even me!

The life I had lived so far was not the life God intended for me to live anymore. Once I realized that His knowledge and understanding surpassed my own, there was very little room for debate. Even if God told me of His ultimate plan, my mind wouldn't even be able to comprehend it. If only I could just believe! Believe not only that Christ was Lord, but that He loved me too. I needed to believe that he had the power to heal me. I learned that he needed me to be exactly where I was, in order to reach me. Everyone has to go through something.

The more we go through things the closer we are to God, because that's when we acknowledge He is God. You see, God wants us to be close to him all the time. God wants us to be in His will and not our own. Sometimes the only time we ask for His guidance and assistance is when our lives are in shambles. When we think things are too much for us to handle, God is already working them out for our good. I learned that it was time now, time for me to face the demons of my past. I knew that medication and therapy wasn't going to be enough. I am not a religious person or by no means a minister. I have no degrees in anything! But it doesn't take a rocket scientist to figure out that when you're seeing things and hearing things, it is bigger than science, bigger than human understanding. No one had to convince me that there was some type of demonic force behind it.

You don't have to believe in God to know that the devil is real. Most people have a better concept of evil than they do of God, or at least I did. I had spent so many years in the grips of evil that it had become a part of me. In my past I had slept with evil, dwelt with it and survived through evil ways. Evil thought it owned me, and was not ready to release me. I was a slave to it. Most people know for themselves of good and evil in the world. To me it was only logical that the turmoil I was in came from the struggle over my soul. Whenever I tried to praise God or read the bible, the visions and voices got louder. They paralyzed me, sending me into seizures and back to hell in my mind. But whenever one of the staff pleaded the blood of Jesus over me, I would come back. Once you have been to the other side and crossed lines that other people haven't crossed, you know the devil wants to keep you hostage. Having seen and done things that most people won't do; whatever the circumstance, whether it was justifiable or not, is irrelevant. The devil wants to hold us hostage to our lust, guilt, vanity, shame, anger, greed, and our behavior!

What other way to go up against a power that is designed to steal, kill and destroy, than with a power that has been around since the beginning of time - the ultimate power. The power that created us; the power that created it, the power that leaves evil deaf, dumb and blind is the power given to me from God! I found the strength to fight this battle through the bible and through Christ who is stronger than me and my mental illness. I learned about a power that lives within me that has freewill and the power of choice. This concept gave me the strength I needed to face each day. I no longer had to wonder if God could love someone like me. When I started to study the bible it taught me that every saint was a sinner. This Christ person in the bible, who gave His life on the cross, did it just for sinners. Which at first I found to be conflicting to my spirit. I started thinking it meant if you're a serial killer or a child molester, then you just say I'm sorry and get to go to heaven. Once again I was pissed off at God and wanted nothing to do with it. Due to the fact that my mental illness handicapped me, I was in and out of the psychiatric hospitals. I couldn't use public bathrooms or even go outside alone.

Sometimes I would revert back to being an infant and could barely walk. Other times I was so sensitive to sound that I would go into seizures, when I heard loud clapping or consistent noise. Anything out of the ordinary would send me over the top. I had to come to the understanding that everyone born in this world is subject to sin. I realized that God, like any loving and caring father, does forgive - but the crime does not go unpunished! Just because God forgives us doesn't mean that there are no consequences for our actions. A lot of people think if you don't forgive your past it will always own you. What I found is that you don't have to forgive. Christians will tell you to forgive the person not the sin. I felt that if you can do that, then you have truly found recovery. As for me, I am only human. I can only forgive at a human capacity. What was done to me was not humane. I am not Christ! I can't forgive what was done to me. Even if I could, I wouldn't want too. I had to do something though. Something that would be okay with me and acceptable to God.

It was evident enough to me that my hate was keeping me in bondage to my past and I desperately wanted to be free. I just couldn't forgive. I started working on conditioning mind and strengthening body. I continued to study the bible, deciding that in the event of war over my soul I needed to become spiritually and physically fit. In order to help God help me I asked other people to pray for me. The staff was very concerned for my mental stability. They comforted me and helped me with my son. I could not have done the work I needed to do without their prayers and support. I started working out and fasting. Trying to find solutions, I found out that I had brain damage to the right side of brain. That's why I struggled with focusing and remembering. I started to wonder how I was going to survive. How was I going to support my son financially? It was suggested to me by my therapist that I re-explore the past. I was very uncomfortable talking about it.

Even after all the work I had done, every time I went back there, I would have a seizure-like episode. So we explored a little at a time. Along with my Christian therapist we called on the Holy Spirit to counsel us, and guide us. When facing my past I tried to identify where God was in my times of trouble. I continued to ask God for help with this. The only answer I received was to go write.

That's when I decided to do this book about my life, so that I could help my mind classify and understand the events of my life. The more I pray, the more I sit in silence, the more God reveals himself to me. The more I work on me and my behavior and perceptions of my reality, the better I get. Suddenly it came to me. If I could not forgive, then I would have to accept what happened to me as testimony. I would have to come to terms with it and let it go.

I would have to go back, step-by-step, giving God every event, every ounce of my pain. I had to surrender my hate towards the people who hurt me. It would mean surrendering my hate towards those who were supposed to protect and shelter me. I didn't have the capacity to forgive them, but I still needed to be free from it, no longer hostage to it. The bible taught me that I could take it to the cross and leave it there with Jesus. There is a God who is full of compassion and understanding who would deal with them in His just and perfect will. I no longer had to carry this burden alone.

There is a power stronger than me who would not let any crime go unpunished. He held me up and carried me even when I didn't believe He was there, He was! Even when I could not see any hope he saved me. I realized that not only did he bring me into the light of good because he loved me, He had a purpose for me and better way of life for me; a life that I never had imagined – full of love and hope. If only I could believe He had the power to heal me, my mind would be restored. Then He could use me to reach the unreachable and touch the hearts of many. I learned to control my anxiety using different breathing techniques. I learned to identify triggers that would send me into those seizures. Working through my past with the therapists showed me that a lot of people in this field of educating the trafficked and mentally ill had very little insight of their realities. I spent a lot of time teaching them about the realities of my world. It was hard for a lot of them to accept that my life was real and that what happened to me was real, that what I was going through was real. I was surprised at their lack of knowledge when it came to exploitation and abduction of children in America. I started to think, what different worlds we come from.

How can people just live and not see what's right there in front of them. I wondered what people think happens to the missing children of the world today. What do people think happens to the children on the milk carton boxes or on the posters? Do they think they have all gone to the moon? Did that make more sense? Are we so caught up in our daily routines and lives that we just choose not to see?

I realized that people didn't want to believe my story because that meant they weren't safe. Their children weren't safe. I realized not many of my predecessors survive to tell their story or to enlighten the world. According to statistics I should have been dead a long time ago. I then realized that it was up to me to educate people. We need to be very cautious of the people we let in our lives. We should teach our children about their surroundings. We need to make sure they're never left unattended. We need to stay all up in their business, being involved in their activities as they mature into young adults. Truth is with cyber space, cell phones and kick apps they don't have to prey on the homeless and the poor anymore. They're in the next room online seeking them out; chatting on line or texting them at the dinner table. The predators are selling them dreams and promising them the world. It is important for us to know what's going on in our children's life.

So, if by chance there are signs, we will see them. If by chance, they start to get lost, we can intervene and help redirect them before they get lost in the turns of life and it's too late. We need to teach them about good and bad; right and wrong. Give them morals and values that say all life is sacred and valuable. There is something wrong in the world that so many men find the exploitation and degradation of women and children attractive.

I realized that when I was young. My life hopes and dreams had been stolen and the people who stole my life were now holding me hostage as an adult. That made me angry, so angry that I wanted revenge! My mind started taking out revenge through my hallucinations. My mind couldn't pretend to be okay with my past anymore. It had nowhere to classify the events of my life when I was a young girl being raped and tortured!

I realized that I sat disassociated from my reality in order to survive it. In order for me to survive in such a hostile environment I adapted to the only realities I knew. That led me through a cycle of life that other people just don't understand. Some don't even acknowledge that it's a reality.

I realized I was a product of my society and I no longer had to be a victim. I needed help with my son and shelter so I went along with the programs rules, giving up my rights and freedom one more time. Once again, it was worth it.

After spending eighteen months in the shelter and in and out of hospitals, staying very active in my own recovery, I started to see things more clearly. It was time to go back out into the world. Time to take my life back, time to obtain the life God would have had me live. It was time for me to step out on faith and trust in God with the assurance that God loves and cares for me. I got on a bus carrying just a few toys for my son, just a few items of clothing and I came here to Detroit. On the bus ride here I felt so alive and human. For the first time in my life I knew that I was finally free at last, free at last! And in divine order of God's will for me. My mind was no longer in turmoil. The anger had completely lifted, the paranoia subsided.

The hallucinations were gone. I have a good relationship with my sister in law and a couple of my brothers. There are still some limitations I have due to the trauma I have suffered. Yes I have had some hard times, no matter, these are certainly the best times of my life. I wouldn't want to imagine a life where I had everything, but never saw the importance of giving. I am no longer just another pretty face cursed with beauty. I am a loving, caring woman whose outer beauty is an introduction to the inner beauty, which is far more precious to me than any diamond or ruby. Much more satisfying and gratifying than the accumulation of things owned. I know that God is preparing a way for me. I will be patient and trust him. Today is my birthday! I am in awe of the miracles God has performed in my life. It is a new beginning!

I know I still have a long way to go. Yet it is good to know how far I have come. It isn't over yet, let's go a little deeper.

~ Ten ~

A Hard Truth

Let's look into why and how these things come about, explore the cause and effects a little further. Let's try to make sense out of nonsense and peace out of mayhem. Let's talk about incest, gangs, exploitation and abusive relationships. I don't want to leave any rocks unturned, because my life depends on sharing the truth in this book. These are the things we won't say or hear in every day passing, but are essential when trying to help someone in these areas. When people are hurt they want answers. So don't quit now; we are we almost done.

Pimpolgy 101

Let us explore the nature of pimps, they are the lowest form of scum on the earth.

They are not men in big hats with fish in their platform boots like you see on television. They are not confined to any one color or gender. They most certainly are not the comical version of men portrayed on television and in the media. There are several layers to the game, or several types of pimps; actually five different classes of pimps.

Class one: The junkie pimp will pimp his girlfriend out for drugs. He is a lower class business pimp and usually a high school dropout who couldn't make it in society. This category also includes parents and relatives who might pimp out their children to make ends meet.

Class two: Second class pimps are usually young poor males whose lives never reached their expectations. So in order for them to provide a lavish lifestyle for themselves, they prey on women and children. They have no aspirations or hopes of making a better life based on their own merit or hard work.

First and second class pimps normally work their girls on the tracks, casinos, truck stops, and escort services. These men also prey on elderly women, heavy set women and lonely women. They trick them into cosigning for them and use their accounts while feeding them lies of desperation or promises of marriage.

Class three: The third class of pimp is the drug dealing pimp who is usually recruited into the game by another pimp's family or by women exploiting themselves for drugs. They are not normally violent to their women but are not against having others hurt them if they feel betrayed or threaten to leave. The catalyst for their involvement is ego and low self-esteem. They usually keep the girls strung out on drugs to control them. In some settings they consider him a 'Mac' which means he has more than one hustle and pimping is secondary.

Class four: The fourth class of pimps own property where they sell women and children. Their properties are disguised as strip clubs, hotels, bath houses and massage parlors.

Class five: Lastly you have the gorilla pimps. They are called that because they snatch their women off the streets, form bus stations, malls, airports and clubs. They are Gangsters disguised as business men. The gorilla pimp is the most dangerous of them all.

All classes of pimps now use the internet to exploit young men and women. This is becoming more and more in demand. Anywhere they can get away with housing and the sale of women and children they will. These pimps usually have some type of job or are in some way connected to society in a way that makes them appear to be productive, like promoters, managers, business owners.

A lot of times girls are sold between pimps, tricked and or blackmailed into staying in the game. Most women are not allowed to just up and leave the game, but can leave one pimp for another. She must buy her way in without his knowledge. The best way to retrieve a girl caught up in the life is to be a pimp. A lot of women come into these places with hopes and dreams of making a quick buck. They may be down on their luck, struggling in school or just trying to feed their children. They don't care about color or class. They prey on whatever it is someone is seeking whether it be friendship, love, fame or fortune.

Now the men who frequent these places have no concern for their well-being or their plans. These men are johns/tricks; average, everyday working class men who live double lives or suffer from fantasy and sex addictions. There is no screening for these men other than the first five minutes of conversation, after that, her life is in his hands. Their only objective is to get whatever they want. Once the door is closed and locked, the woman or child is pretty much at his mercy. This is the gateway for much more abuse and even murder. These men have no one to answer to for what they do other than the pimp who is nowhere around when the acts are being committed. The pimp's job is to keep them in the game as long as possible through manipulation, drugs or force. If a minor is caught with one of these men, he is not arrested because she is not considered a victim but the predator in our society. Their acts of violence against their victims are calculated, malicious and intentional. Like any other pedophile, pimps hate women.

When a man hates women, and a woman gave him life, the question that comes to mind for me is - does he really desire another man instead of a woman and is just too much of a coward to admit his own truth? When a man hates women, it's because he despises himself. These men have no values or morals and to him, women are dispensable. They think women only exist to meet their needs so they prey on innocent children – boys, girls and lonely women. It is slavery! The victims are being manipulated, raped and beaten. Their families and children's lives threatened. There is no honor or glory in this type of thinking that somehow makes another human beings life expendable.

Yet in our society we applaud this behavior and idolize these men in front of our youth through media, television and radio as if they are great achievers. We tap them on the hand and say you better not do that again, excusing the realities of these men who lack discipline and character. We can no longer afford to allow these "victims of circumstances" or a man "born poor, uneducated, abused whatever the case that made them feel less than a man" as an excuse for this type of inhumane behavior.

They did, with good conscience, set out to destroy another human's life and took pride in doing so. This makes them less than a man if anything.

The media portrays them as God-like, when in reality they are closer to animals than most. If it lives like an animal and acts like an animal, then it is an animal. These men seek out the weakest, most vulnerable beings on the planet. Then justify it by throwing money at their feet. Like a wolf seeking out a sheep or a lion seeking out a deer, it is animalistic to say the least.

The young girls and boys who fall into the traps of predators like this sometimes die horrible deaths. Their customers or their pimp may kill them before they find a way out. They may be in slavery for years before they figure out that it's wrong. Shame and guilt won't let them go home or search for a way out. There is very little help out there addressing this issue. It is becoming a bigger and bigger problem, with more and more ways to violate and exploit children. And it is happening now more than ever in America. Ask yourself, how does one recover from being a human toilet?

There are more predators stalking our children, in our schools, on our computers. Trying to buy and sell our children. This is big business in America. Police, politicians, teachers, lawyers, athletes, movie stars, judges and regular businessmen are the prime clients of the sale! Yet we look the other way and we blame the victims and label them whores, drug addicts and faggots. Those drug addicts, whores and faggots are someone's children; sister or brother.

It is a very hard way to live for the victim and the predator. A person must be spiritually numb and emotionally detached in order to survive. The slightest sign of vulnerability could have cost me my life. After being conditioned to live like this, I died to who I was in order to survive. Every time I stepped into a car or a back room with one of these customers, my life was at stake. No one can trust anyone, at any time, for any reason. They're being raped and beaten by the johns and the pimps every day. They have nowhere to turn.

The pimp doesn't understand the qualities it takes to be a real man. He can't be in a real relationship. So he takes it out on the women or men in his life that find him exciting or interesting. He has no real attraction to the opposite sex. It is all about the control and the game. It is easy for him to do things that the average man would never consider doing to his or her partner. They dream of being with a successful intelligent woman, but they know that they could never live up to her standards. So they prey on the weak, vulnerable and the innocent. A lot of them have issues where their own childhood is concerned. They were neglected, abused, or were never good enough. Inside they feel weak and insignificant.

We need to teach our men the value of life; the pride in a dollar earned and a dollar saved. The value of women; we need to teach them that men are supposed to cherish, protect, and help provide for their families; for their women. We need to bring back family values, and God's law. We need to teach our men to look to themselves, and to trust God.

<u>Incest and rape</u>:

Incest and rape are the most heinous of crimes. It's a very touchy subject that most people would prefer not to talk about. Some of the crimes against children today are being ignored or looked over. In a lot of cases it is still being swept under the rug. This is a serious epidemic and should not be taken lightly. Predators have no remorse for what they do to innocent children. Seven years in prison is a far cry from any type of real justice. The reality is, they actually only do half of the time they are sentenced. The aftercare consists of some minor probation, which is just reporting to an over-loaded case manager once a month. People who are convicted of violent crimes against children should have to do all their time in jail, 100%. If there was a death penalty against perpetrators, there would be a lot less crimes against children being committed. A life for a life is the only justice fitting the crime. I realize that's wishful thinking and probably highly unrealistic, but can we at least shoot for more than a couple of years.

Victims of rape and incest spend a whole lifetime in recovery over what has been done to them. They suffer from guilt and shame, thinking somehow this is their fault. It's like having your life snatched out from under your feet. One moment you are a young and innocent child, roller skating and hanging out at the park. The next moment your life just stops, and you're dead inside, suffering from fear, severe low self-esteem, suicidal tendencies, anger and rage or even homicidal tendencies. Some will spend thousands on therapy. Some will have to be medicated just to function. Some will even become predators themselves. Their reality becomes distorted. This crime not only assaults the body but the mind and the spirit as well. You're looking for reasons the people who are supposed to care for you and protect you, hurt you. Grownups are responsible to help nurture and care for any child they come in contact with, not just their own. Grownups need to be accountable for their actions. Some questions have no answers, but here are some answers to some questions that I have found useful. This does not justify the action. It is just for clarification of the excuses.

- People do what they have been taught
- Some parents look the other way for fear of being alone
- Some predators have been victims themselves
- A perverse spirit (Demonic Spirit)

Healing begins with prayer, intervention, and lots of therapy! The victims have to learn to rebuild a confidence in self and trust in the people around them. I do not have to stay imprisoned in the past. I do not have to let people, places and things that are out of my control own me. I am the ruler of my thoughts and emotions and I can learn to control them. I can learn to think with logic and reason. There is a right and a wrong way to deal with pain. It's not what happens to us that defines us. It's what we do in life and how we react to situations. It's how we treat ourselves and others that determines what our legacies will be.

Signs of an abused child:

- Anger
- Acting out
- Isolation
- Constant bathing
- Doesn't want to come home
- Doesn't want you to leave
- Fear
- Bed wetting
- Eating disorders

They are not in any order and may not all apply to every child. They are just some of the things I suffered with as a child.

Gangs:

Being in a gang gave me security. I felt powerful around them. We all knew it was wrong to hurt people. You could smell guilt and shame in the air whenever we were together. Gangs were not intended to be a cesspool for genocide. They were formed to protect inner city neighborhoods against the KKK and pedophiles and police brutality. They were to be a force that would protect schools and children from the very things they are being afflicted by today. They were designed to demonstrate order within the communities, rally for the same opportunities that other children got. They were to build alliances with other gangs that were about business so that they could buy their own businesses and employ people within the inner cities.

Somewhere along the way the concept got forgotten. Drugs were being shipped into the neighborhoods. Liquor stores were being opened from corner to corner. It was a trap that was set in place to break a people! The world was too afraid to see a united black people in those times. Times have changed, but our children can't see a future. So we turn to the only things we feel will give them a way out by capitalizing on what's in front and all around us. We dislike their lives so much that we want to destroy anything that reflects us. Their visions of success in America have been distorted to a recipe of self-hate, sentencing them to death and prison. Now they kill each other to feel worthy, not understanding that they are only contributing to the hypocrisy and poverty in which they live in.

Saving up to do life in the penitentiary! We call ourselves gangsters yet we are doing nothing to secure our futures or the futures of those coming up behind us. We are not gangsters, just lost, confused individuals. We are a people still in bondage that have no hope of a civil future. We are products of our environment. How can someone who has never seen civil society envision a life for themselves in one? Shelters all across the country are filled with women and children who can't afford housing and food. Busy streets are flooded with young women and men trading souls for a moment of instant gratification via drugs, alcohol, sex, gambling whatever - anything goes. We are still a people in bondage.

Look at President Barack Obama, Rev. Martin Luther King Jr., Malcolm X, Farrakhan or Nelson Mandela. Now they are what I call real gangsters and the rest of us need to step up the game. They have and had purpose; a meaning, a cause and their legacy is worth leaving. They are real men who will not be remembered for genocide but for the contributions they made to society. If our young men view men as gangsters hero's, then it is up to us to smash the illusion that gangsters are killers, thieves, rapists and lost. It is up to us to change their perception of what a gangster is about.

Who am I? We as individuals who can see past what is right in front of us need to start caring for others who don't know how too, or can't care for themselves, until they learn too.

Relationships:

Relationships take two people giving and taking equally. I am not saying that a relationship has to be 100% all the time. I am saying if you start at 100%, at worst you're at 50% and still have half a chance. That works both ways. If you're the only one in love, then you're not in a relationship. Every relationship is about giving and taking. When you're taking more than you're giving, you're the reason for the hostile environment you live in.

If you're giving more than you're taking in a relationship, you are not a victim, you're volunteering to be a doormat. You're the reason there is nothing left for yourself. In my opinion, a couple should spend at least twenty minutes a day in conversation. In a relationship it is important to keep the lines of communication open

The bible is clear on relationships and again, a great guide. We should love one another as we love ourselves. Very good concept actually. Key words are – "as we love ourselves". Without acquiring self-love there cannot be a healthy relationship. We become open targets to be used, abused and stepped on. We have to be sure not to mistake our self-pride, self-centeredness, and boastfulness, for self-love. There is a big difference.

A great way to learn how to be in a relationship is by having relationships with God, with ourselves and our families. Then, go out and get a plant or a bird before we get to a significant other or decide to have children with someone.

The order of things is important. Without having a

relationship with God, ourselves and family, it would be highly unlikely to have a healthy, stable, and intimate relationship with anyone. For instance, if a person never has had a healthy relationship with their parents, they will spend years trying to fill that void, chasing the dream of that relationship.

The fact is there is no one who can live up to the expectations of that dream. It is a ridiculous expectation. Obviously not even our parents can. So why would we expect someone else to do what they couldn't? How do we fill that void? Well, if they're still living, those of us who put other people on pedestals - please stop. Think about it, if they are perfect then what does that make us, average? The fact is, no one is perfect. We are all human beings born in sin and prisoners of our flesh. If it's a person you're looking too that will meet all your expectations then you may never find a mate.

Don't misconstrue what I'm saying. There is a perfect match for us. There are just not any perfect people. If we decide to have a relationship, we need to recognize that prior to going into one, so just in case - if by chance they lie, cheat, steal, abuse us or take us for granted - we won't be absolutely crushed.

When we are deceived or when someone decides to smash our perfect picture of life, you can trust that there is a very good chance that at some point in our lives we will get hurt by someone we decided to be involved with. Pain is pain no matter how it comes. We should recognize that it is just an experience and it is through personal experiences that we gain wisdom to make better decisions. When we have other healthy relationships in our lives, we get over it more easily! We read signs of abuse more accurately. We have boundaries in place that will protect us from being violated, taken advantage of or robbed in the future. Even in the event those things happen to us anyway, we move on more quickly. We forgive more easily. We should have high standards when it comes to choosing a life partner; but not unreasonable ones. Our expectations should be practical and spiritual. The primary goals in life should be mutual. She should be your cold glass of water on a hot summer's day. He should be your heated blanket on a cold winter night.

Caution signs

- Pointing out your flaws
- Calling you names
- Telling you how to dress
- Telling you who your friends should be
- Getting mad when you want space
- Searching your phone, personal belongings
- Constantly accusing you of lying or cheating
- Speaking for you
- Being violent to other people
- Living a double life

In this day and age, it is absolutely necessary to talk about sex prior to having sex. The bible is very clear on pre-marital sex for those of us who choose to have sexual relations outside of marriage. We need to take precautions when choosing a lover. It is always better to let the other person know who you are. It gives them the option to say yes or no; that is very important. Especially true if you are sexually active with someone else at the time you meet a new lover; also if you are gay or bi-sexual. Honesty is hard for a lot of people. What is the point of getting into a relationship if the goal is not marriage?

Honesty is necessary though. Honesty brings freedom to relationships. Freedom to be yourself. Some people spend a lifetime caught up in lies or living double lives when all they need to do is be honest. Honest to themselves and their lovers. No one knows what you want unless you tell him or her. I think doing background checks is important. You might save yourself some unnecessary pain if you do so. Please make sure that before you have unprotected sex you get a checkup. Every time you meet a new lover you become high risk. The ultimate responsibility for my safety belongs to me. Sex is not a relationship, just a form of instant gratification. It is not a sign of power but of weakness, weakness of the flesh.

There is much more power in discipline. It doesn't take a mature person to have sex. It takes a lot more courage to apply restraints to sexual urges than it does to be sexually open. Why take the risk? Instant gratification is not a cure for anything. As a matter a fact it is a sure way to get your feelings hurt.

It is only when you become husband and wife that sex is okay in the eyes of God. If there isn't a real desire for both parties to achieve something greater and lasting, you may very well just be wasting time. That is why it is important to accept the reality, so you're not investing more than you're willing to lose. What I try to remember is that self-discipline and telling myself no, is real power. Anything worth having is worth waiting for and working towards. If you're wondering where this topic came from or why someone like me would have an opinion on relationships – read on.

Fifteen years of civil service to the husbands of America, and the derelicts of the world is about the equivalent of a doctorate. Nine years of recovery and personal growth is about the equivalent of a psychiatrist. For those with no sense of humor, that's called comic relief! Take it for what it's worth.

The sun is going to shine with or without me, no matter my situation or my feelings about them. Ultimately the choice is mine and I choose to shine with the sun on a daily basis. Live, love and enjoy your life. It is the only one you have. Remain teachable. If the process of life is growth, and I'm not learning something, then I merely exist or am just surviving.

I am so grateful for the people who reached out and touched me. They showed me the strength and courage that I needed to be vigilant in my personal recovery, if by chance my story reaches you; I pray that you will be blessed! If you're wondering where my happy ending is; it is somewhere between soaring through the storms of life and riding on the wings of our Lord, the sovereign Christ Jesus!

I know that there is a God and He loves me too!

~ Eleven ~

Food for Thought

The Trafficked:

There is no such thing as a child prostitute. Not even if they have been tricked, coerced or forced into believing that their body is for sale, rent or hire. Not even if they did it willingly, to get a new pair of shoes or to gain some type of favor. A person under the age of 18 should never be looked at or referred to in such a way. They have been taken advantage of by someone much older who found their weakness and used it against them. This should not be acceptable; it is still rape.

Here in America, a grown man can be caught having sex with a minor. If they are homeless, abandoned, ward of the court or a runaway, they become criminalized, labeled a prostitute. The man, on the other hand, gets a warning and is sent home to his children. This is where we have failed so many in our society. To suggest that because of their circumstance they are no longer human beings, thereby making it acceptable to exploit them, is downright brutality. Sadly, we have accepted this as normal in our society. Maybe we convinced ourselves it was okay as long as it is not happening in our homes or our neighborhoods. When the times changed, the game changed. Predators no longer have to search the ghettos for the homeless and less fortunate. They are in chat rooms, on the phones and internet of children all over the country. Cyber space is the door most commonly used. In today's society anyone and everyone has the potential to be preyed upon.

There is no such thing as a sex worker, a happy hooker or prostitute. The myth is that she somehow volunteered to sell herself, day after day, month after month and year after year, used as a human garbage can for the fun of it. She signed up to be beaten, robbed, degraded and raped up to 10 or 15 times a day. She could be murdered at any given moment and she somehow enjoys it. Imagine having sex that many times a day with someone you love. Then imagine how quickly you would come to hate it. They are definitely not the majority, even if they're 5 out of a thousand it's a small number. To believe anything more defies rational thought.

Some have convinced themselves that the life is acceptable and beneficial. It is a mask worn to protect themselves. In this lifestyle there is no room for doubt. Doubt leaves them vulnerable with a target on their back. Dreaming of something different is not wise. Shame and guilt can consume them to the point of suicide. The mask must not only fool society, but themselves as well. The mask is the only weapon of defense they truly have. They simply do not believe there is any other way of life they would be accepted in. Whether they have been tricked, coerced or forced as a child or even as a grownup, it is still trafficking. Through desperation, poverty, drugs, man or entity, it is still wrong. They are human beings who deserve compassion.

If a psychologist rapes his client it is wrong. If a teacher rapes their student it is wrong. So why should men with money, property and prestige be able to seek out those less fortunate or naive and rape them? Then they justify it by throwing money at their feet. Where is the humanity in that? Healing takes time. And those who have been forced into the life need healing. Just food for thought.

~~The end~~ The Beginning

Alice Jay ...

...is more than a survivor. She is an advocate, friend and powerful facilitator for freedom for victims of human trafficking. She is passionate about assisting women who have suffered this trauma. She knows that once freed, many girls are unable to live productive lives.

After living through 20 years of imprisonment, Alice volunteers as a consultant on human trafficking with the FBI to infiltrate this billion dollar industry. She has also served on several panels and works with State Representatives in Michigan to stop the criminalization of minors, get help for minors being trafficked as well as getting healthcare and therapy for all survivors.

Alice is a speaker, teacher, facilitator, motivator and voice of experience. She believes many organizations who would support victims of human trafficking are well meaning, however, "They've never been there so they are missing important elements to be effective."

Survivor, Advocate, Facilitator, Mother

Alice Jay is the proud mother of two children.

Connect with Alice via:

Email: alicejohnson7790@yahoo.com
FB: groups/voicespeak

CPSIA information can be obtained
at www.ICGtesting.com
Printed in the USA
BVHW04s2139110818
523998BV00007B/134/P

9 781937 400484